OFF-BALANCE

Judge Connor

&

Karen

OFF-BALANCE

A Humorous View of
Heartland America
from the Bench of a District Court Judge

Judge John L. Conover

Karen D. Conover

To order additional copies, please visit:

www.judgeconover.com

Cover Photo of Judge John L. Conover used by permission from MLIVE.COM/Landov

Back cover photo of Karen Conover used by permission from Photo Factory, USA, Inc. Davison, MI

Usage licenses have been properly purchased for all other photos and clip art except for those personally produced by the authors.

Cover design: Will Davis

We have been greatly blessed
with a loving and caring family.
We dedicate this book
with all of our love
To our daughter Bree, her husband Scott,
To their children: Lilian, Miriam and Oscar;
To our son Chad, his wife Julie and
To their children: Brandon, Ciera and Zoe.
—John

To family who came before us;
To friends who came alongside;
To our children who have enriched our journey;
To grandchildren who carry us forward.
—Karen

INTRODUCTION

I live my professional life suspended and blended between Normal Rockwell America and what has often been named the most violent city in the United States.

I've had the privilege and honor of sitting as a District Court Judge for twenty-one years. My voting district includes several small, mostly rural or suburban communities which I would characterize as typically Midwestern Americana. However, my jurisdiction includes all the areas in the county of Genesee which lie outside the city of Flint, Michigan. Flint, you may know, has been infamously named by the FBI as the most dangerous city in America (often even ranking ahead of Detroit!!) because of the percentage of homicides and violent crimes compared to its population size...not winning this "honor" once, but in several recent years. Naturally, city borders do not restrict such crime from spilling over into areas of my jurisdiction.

I work in an amazing microcosm of America itself. Many Americans (though they are mostly ignored...or slandered, by the pop culture and media) live in relative peace and modest prosperity where they send their children to safe schools and strive to make a better life for themselves and their children. That's where I live and preside over its court. But then there is the "other" America. It is dank and crumbling and riddled with failure. Many families are unraveled there. Too many children bounce among relatives and foster homes, and one out of seven of them is abused or neglected [recent statistics from the Flint Whaley Home for Children and Protective Services]. Schools there flounder in near hopelessness to even fight illiteracy, let alone to provide students with the more advanced technology and higher cognitive skills for future success. Unemployment rages in these dying cities (officially claimed to be around seventeen percent in our area…a number many locals would claim to be highly underestimated). Tens of thousands of workers in the entire Genesee area have lost jobs in manufacturing since the year 2000, either finding no work at all or lower-paying employment. In the area of Flint, once one of the foremost auto manufacturing centers in the world, the proportion of people living in poverty now hovers around twenty-five percent: literally one out of every four people. Young people between 18 and 35 are unemployed at even more staggering rates, well above that of the general population, mainly because many do not have meaningful high school degrees (meaning they can competently read and write) nor do they possess other employable skills now that the auto plants are gone.

Amazingly, these two worlds exist only minutes apart by car. I make that trip several times a week as I work between the suburban, small city courthouse in Davison and the Genesee County Courthouse in Flint. The cases I hear in Davison are usually tame, to say the least, compared to the often violent crime cases I hear in the county court. I have been known to hear a miner shoplifting case, some landlord/tenant disputes, and a dog running loose charge in Davison one day, and the next day preside over a small child's torturous and sickening murder case in the Genesee County Courthouse. In Davison, citizens drive, walk, and shop in relative safety. Ten minutes away, such activities are not always taken for granted as being comfortably safe ventures.

Some day I might write a book about the terrible things I've seen in my experience on the bench, but I doubt it. One only needs to read the newspaper or watch television news to know about the sad and painful situations that haunt the lives of so many of our fellow citizens. Tragedies, and stories about the tragedies that we and others endure, seep into all our lives whether or not we choose to dwell on those facts. Adding more specific gore to those sad accounts will certainly not enhance anyone's lives.

On the brighter side, as a judge I've had the opportunity to help positively redirect the lives of many people. I choose to focus on that instead of seeing myself as a dispenser of "justice." Justice belongs exclusively to God. My job is to administer just enough punishing medicine (not too little, not too much) to force that defendant to see the error of his/her ways. Sadly, it doesn't always work and some defendants take their punishment and turn around and double down on stupid, continuing their downward spiral. I rejoice in those who, instead, take their punishment and turn their lives around, and I cherish each and every letter or note from those people who credit me with re-directing their lives. Short of endangering the public or the welfare of the defendant's family, I try to give offenders every opportunity to "see the light."

I also have made a point to see the humor in life...wherever it can be found. I credit my father with that ability. He was a bright and witty man whose youth was spent fighting his way out of the Depression, yet he could see the humor in the darkest of problems. He made me laugh, sometimes even at my own expense.

I also credit my wife, Karen, who can turn real life stories into literary gems of humor. My stories are funny, but she can describe them with her creative vocabulary and Mark Twain-style humor to make them even funnier.

So, here is a collection of real life stories which span my whole career on the bench, including some that go back to when I was an upstart lawyer. I would always write down the more amusing events that happened around me in the criminal justice world and use them in my frequent community speeches. I soon accumulated stacks of yellow notepads with story after story on them.

One day, my wife and I decided that she would take the stories and creatively re-write them. The stories are all basically factual. Some dialog has been re-created after many years and therefore, not all the quotes are historically word-for-word. However, every story portrays the spirit of the actual event. Some literary license has been used about the facts in the stories, but very little. Names have been changed in almost every case, but not all.

We sincerely hope you enjoy this amusing collection of American life as seen from the viewpoint of my bench...with a magic touch from my wife's keyboard.

In the first months of my tenure on the bench, I was asked to perform a wedding. Of all the weddings I've performed since then, that first one was indeed the most memorable!

It all began when my court reporter, Toni, came wide-eyed into my chambers to tell me that the bride had arrived. The bride, WELL ADVANCED IN YEARS, came fully dressed in a white lace bridal gown with her middle-age granddaughters fluttering around her. Clerks, secretaries, city workers, and the cops across the hall were all stealing glances at this very unconventional bride and running for closets to muffle their laughter. She truly looked like Charles Dickens' character, Miss Haversham (who was dumped on her wedding day and didn't take off her wedding dress for the next fifty years), come to life in my courtroom.

The groom, of even more advanced years, arrived looking disheveled and confused. His family, undaunted, had clearly already begun the liquid festivities.

I proudly gathered the happy couple and their entourage

into my courtroom. I had spent hours studying various wedding ceremonies and coming up with the "perfect" one! Then I had rehearsed my part until I felt confident in my new role. To preserve the historic event, I had pressed my reluctant wife into serving as videographer.

Everything went according to plan even when I stumbled when I asked the aged groom: "Do you, Clarence, take Mary to be your *awfully* wedded wife…etc.?" Fortunately Clarence's hearing aid filtered out my blunder and things progressed.

Then I turned to Mary and asked: "Do you, Mary, take Clarence to be your *lawfully* wedded husband…etc?" Mary stared at Clarence and didn't respond. The silence lengthened embarrassingly. I began to worry that Mary also had a hearing problem so I loudly repeated myself.

Silence.

Finally I decided to defuse the moment and teased our lace-bedecked octogenarian: "Mary! I can tell by the look in Clarence's eyes that he is ready to get married today! Do I need to go down to *Archie's* (our local family diner) and find a bride for him?" Mary looked thoughtful, then said: "Oh, okay!"

Relieved, I forged on through the wrap-up and proudly proclaimed: "Clarence, you may kiss the bride!" At which point, the surprisingly spry bride grabbed me and planted a pruney kiss squarely on *my* mouth! My wife nearly dropped the video camera in laughter, and a raucous grandson shouted: "Kiss him again, Grandma, so I can get a picture!"

As quickly as I could, I got papers signed and rounded up the wedding party and steered them to the door. I politely declined the invitation to join the ensuing reception even though the happy crowd insisted that my wife and I would be welcome.

"Oh Judge!" the Grandson shouted back from the door: "There's plenty of kegs to go around….!"

I sometimes perform informal weddings in the courtroom between other court business, if the couple doesn't object.

These weddings are usually quick and casual, but one
such wedding surprised me when the bride showed up in full
white wedding gown with several "trappings." It also surprised
the spectators and those waiting on court business in the half-
full courtroom.

The bride's dress was borrowed (evidently from a lady far
less endowed) and was VERY tight...and strapless. The busty
bride appeared to be tenuously stuffed within the lacy fabric.
She also appeared to be dangerously uncomfortable and, indeed,
did complain of not feeling well.

Partway through the vows, the bride's eyes rolled back in
her head and she passed out cold. The maid-of-honor caught her
as she fell backwards and, in an act of apparent mercy, began to
unzip the too-small bridal gown.

Just like opening a can of refrigerated
biscuits, the bride exploded out of the un-
natural compression of her dress, allowing her to breathe, but also providing an
X-rated view of her considerable assets
to friend and stranger alike.

Now able to breathe, the bride came to. The groom gallantly
covered what he could with a small square of pocket hanky. The
maid-of-honor stuffed what she could back in the dress and held
it up, along with the bride, with grim determination.

The vows were finished and the entire family assisted the
groom in carrying his new bride feet-first out of the courtroom,
the maid-of-honor still unsuccessfully trying to turn this into a
G-rated event as she clutched at the gown's fabric.

When the doors swung shut behind the marital entourage, I looked around at the remaining gaping attorneys and stunned citizens who were awaiting their day in court and said: "Folks, I think we all need a fifteen minute break after that stirring ceremony….Is it hot in here?"

Landlord/tenant cases are never pleasant. The landlord is losing money, and the tenants fear losing their home. In a recent case from a large apartment complex, I had both the tenant and the apartment manager stand up and each tell me their side of the story. Based on their testimony, and a failed attempt at settlement, I ordered the eviction of the tenant.

After giving my decision, the parties continued to glare at each other with an unusual amount of animosity.

"Do you two know each other?" I inquired.

Disgustedly, the manager said: "She's my mother-in-law!"

"You evicted your mother-in-law?" I asked incredulously. "Wow! Thanksgiving is coming up. Are you two planning a family get-together?"

"She'll probably be living with us," the manager grumbled under his breath.

"Hummm," I replied. "Who's cooking the turkey….?"

"What in the world were you thinking?"

These are words that I have frequently expressed during my twenty-one years as a district court judge. More often than not, they come from sheer amazement rather than from legal curiosity.

I aimed this exact question at a female convenience store clerk who had been robbed. The perpetrators, two women with obvious environmental concerns, had brought their own "green bags" into the store and proceeded to casually saunter throughout the store, filling the bags with bread, milk, beer and a mix of other items. The clerk was not alarmed until the "ladies" approached the checkout counter. One woman suddenly pulled a gun out of her purse and demanded that the cash register be opened and all the cash be dumped on top of the food in their bags!

The clerk complied as was the store policy and also because it seemed to be the best way to live to see another day. After stuffing the money into their already full green bags, the robbers dashed for the door...actually running into one another in their haste...and spilling some of the cash, food...and food stamps (at that time still in paper coupon form) from their bags!

Then came the compounded craziness: the unarmed clerk reported to me in court that she then chased the gun-wielding robbers, yelling: "Stop! Ladies, please stop! You dropped your bread, cookies and food stamps!"

The clerk's response to my "What were you thinking?" question was "I guess I was just trying to be polite."

Was she following some phantom chapter in *Miss Manners* on Victim Etiquette?

In all fairness, the robbers in this Miss Manners case were equally polite. They didn't, for instance, shoot her dead or commit battery (legal talk for beating her senseless) as she chased after them. I guess you could say they were very considerate.

And in a gracious act, which saved the police and prosecutors a lot of trouble identifying and arresting the culprits: among the dropped items the robbers left behind were the traceable food stamp coupons which led police right to their door and their stuffed green bags!

Now there's civility!

Evidently criminals often depend on polite victims to aid in their crimes. Another armed robber ran into a very civil victim, a woman manager of a mall department store.

The robber, having entered the department store, browsed for a few minutes, and then asked for the store manager. From casing the store previously, he knew that there was a safe in the manager's office which he hoped contained a substantial amount of money.

The perpetrator had covered a 9 mm gun with an overcoat on his arm. When he had steered the manager to an area of the store where he claimed to have a question for her, he suddenly stuck the gun in the manager's back and ordered her into her office. The terrified manager complied.

Once secreted in her office he told the manager: "I will kill you unless you do two things. First, unlock the safe and give me all the money. Secondly, you're going to give me a ten minute head start. You are not going to call 911 and you are not going to talk to *anyone* until that ten minutes is up!" In terror, she quickly and wisely agreed to his terms.

After taking about $1,000 from the safe, the robber reminded the manager of her promise, closed her in the office, and then fled the mall.

Other employees saw the man run out of the manager's office and rushed to her aid, assuming the worst. She let them in, but refused to tell them what had happened or allow them to call the police. She frantically looked at the clock and blurted out: "I can't talk for eight more minutes!"

Arms folded, lips pinched and trembling, the manager refused all pleas for information, only continuing to cite the time remaining: "I can't talk for five more minutes!" No amount of questioning could get her to say anything else. Finally, she looked at her watch and counted down the last few seconds: "...four, three, two, one!" Then she jumped up and screamed: "We've just been robbed!! Call 911!!"

What was she thinking? She evidently saw no inconsistency in keeping her word to a thug who would rob her safe and threaten her very life...even with him completely gone!

This must be another chapter of the phantom book on Victim Etiquette!

A lso among quirky robberies falls the story of two women who were charged with unarmed robbery.

The women had gone into a party store with larceny on their minds—but did they steal money or Milk Duds? Maybe a bottle of booze? No, they slipped into the storage room with a large garbage bag and stuffed the bag with returnable pop and beer cans, then ran out to a small car and sped away.

The two gangster mamas were arrested about three miles away in the parking lot of another party store where they were going to cash in the cans and bottles. An officer pulled up to the small car over-stuffed with two large women and two large bags of returnable pop and beer cans.

"Really, Officer," they insisted: "we picked these up along the highway!"

"Okay." replied the officer: "Which highway?"

Simultaneously, in perfect vaudeville comedy style, one said: "I-69." The other said "I-75."

Victims aren't the only transgressors of the "What were you thinking?" question. Brash young lawyers often get my "look" which communicates the same question.

A novice defense attorney had evidently been watching too many dramatized TV court trials. He strutted importantly and harassed an elderly lady witness in an effort to get her to "admit" that the prosecution had coached her to lie on the stand. Pouncing on this imaginary bone, he demanded dramatically: "Tell this jury what *exactly* the prosecutor told you about being cross-examined by me!"

The elderly witness turned scarlet with embarrassment, and with a touch of anger. Then after looking at me, she blurted out: "He said you would be an upstart pain in the butt!"

The courtroom exploded in laughter.

What was he thinking? This young attorney broke the cardinal rule of cross-examining tactics (the same one Attorney Christopher Darden broke in the legendary O.J. Simpson trial when he challenged Simpson to try on the bloody glove): "Never ask a question in front of a jury or judge to which you aren't pretty sure of the answer."

Movies have been depicting criminal brilliance for decades. Sorry, *Spiderman* movie fans, I have found that the vast majority of criminals are more dopey than daring, more stupid than diabolical.

On a beautiful Fall Sunday in Michigan, two young men missed church and took it into their pea-brain heads to rob a local sports bar at gunpoint.

After breaking through an outside entrance into the bar's basement and forcing the manager (who had gone down to check on the suspicious noise) to unlock the safe, a dim light flickered in their minds that the bar should be filled with patrons watching NFL football and they could further increase their ill-gotten booty with billfolds, purses and watches!

In that hope, they tied up the manager, then burst into the bar, guns drawn...only to find one drunk with his head on the bar, one startled bartender, and several blaring TVs.

The robbers were stunned! They expected the bar to be filled with NFL fans on a Sunday afternoon! While they stood there in confused hesitation, the police who had been summoned by the manager's silent security alarm arrived on the scene, and the duo ended up facing me in orange jumpsuits.

Before dispensing justice, I asked the two geniuses if they knew where their plan had gone wrong. When my question only elicited sullen shrugs, I pointed out the obvious: the sports bar was empty because the Detroit Lions were playing....

S peaking of Mensa Society rejects, three men dressed in black rode their bikes into a subdivision to rob a home while the residents were in Flori-

da. It was dusk when they rode up to the house and a neighbor, returning a tool to his shed, observed the three men sneak their bikes up his friends' driveway.

What caught his attention? The three brainiacs, who had carefully dressed in camouflage black, were also wearing fluorescent orange hunting hats!

Now there's a stroke of genius.

S ometimes the plan goes wrong for police officers too. When our son was in police academy, he had a range instructor who was a steely drill sergeant.

On the first day of the class's range drill, half of the cadets approached the firing line while our son and the rest of his group waited their turn. The instructor barked out drill orders which the cadets were instructed to carry out as quickly as possible.

The group did fine when the order was to "LOAD!" The cadets quickly loaded their guns. However, when the instructor barked: "UNLOAD!" instead of quickly cracking the chamber and removing the bullets from his gun as the instructor had outlined before the maneuver, one confused cadet began rapid-firing at the target, and the rest of the group quickly followed suit in a thunderous explosion as they emptied their full chambers at the range targets.

As the fire died away, the instructor stood dumbstruck for a full beat, then said dryly: "Before I begin handing out demerits for stupidity, I want to compliment everyone on the *speed* of that last maneuver."

There was no confusion on the part of a long-time township officer when he appeared before me to seek an arrest warrant for a person shoplifting meat from a local grocery store. When I asked him how the defendant was caught, the officer, straight-faced, replied: "From a STEAK-out, Sir."

I'm actually a great admirer of the bravery so often demonstrated by our law enforcement officers (hat tip to son Chad). On a bitter winter day one of our young officers responded to a 911 call to find a man whose dog had fallen through the ice

of a small pond and had been struggling for several minutes to stay alive. The ice wouldn't hold his weight, but he couldn't break enough of it to clear a path to shore. It was clear that the dog would soon lose his battle and his life.

Without hesitation the officer waded into the pond, breaking the ice as he went and finally swimming to get the dog and pull him out of the frigid water.

This young officer saw a crisis and responded without thought for his own safety. I enjoy teasing him (erroneously) that I heard that he gave the dog mouth-to-mouth resuscitation.

It's my back-handed way of complimenting his brave act.

Some officers, of course, have dogs that serve with them. These canine officers are often in danger, arriving at active crime scenes where quick and accurate action is paramount.

A young officer and his dog were dispatched to a robbery in progress at a party store. As the policeman pulled into the parking lot, three men ran out of the party store and into the night. Leaving his dog in the car, the officer began chasing the robbers when they suddenly stopped at a high fence and turned threateningly on the officer and began to chase him down.

The way this is supposed to work is that the canine officer carries a remote device that he activates to open the door of his squad car to release the dog. Unfortunately, in this situation, the young officer had forgotten to release the dog and he soon outran his remote's activation area. He was beyond where he could release the dog.

Seeing the pickle that he had created for himself, the officer started running at top speed *back* toward the car, robbers in hot pursuit of him, frantically pushing the remote. When he neared the car, the robbers turned again and tried to scale the fence.

By the time he escaped the car, the dog was at full adrenaline and full speed. With a few surgical chomps on their backsides, the dog made short work of corralling the thieves…with a little help from his human partner who had learned some very important lessons that night.

Namely: next time, don't forget to let the dogs out! Bark!

GRRRRRRRR…

A drunk driver also needed to be rescued by police and paramedics. He missed a curve and drove his car straight into Picnic Lake. I told him that next time he's driving on a road near Picnic Lake, he should wear a life jacket and have along an inflatable picnic basket.

It's my policy to temper justice with as much common sense as possible. I try to approach cases as an Everyman.

A young man was charged with urinating in a public place and appeared in front of me. I learned that the defendant was driving home from a friend's, had not been drinking, had been standing behind a billboard...about 2 A.M...out on a country road! Now that's a long stretch for the long arm of the law, even for our fine officers! (And, of course, you wonder why the officer was stopped in sight of the back of that billboard....)

The young man pled guilty, and during the course of discussing a possible sentence, I said: "I doubt, young man, if there is a person in this courtroom who, at some time or another, has not had to urinate somewhere in the great outdoors."

At that, the prosecuting attorney jumped up and blurted out: "Your Honor, I want you to know that *I* never have!"

"Well," I smiled at her, "you really need to get out more.

"Case dismissed."

The long arm of the law reached another errant citizen who was arrested and being arraigned in my court.

"Well, Mr. Jones," I began: "why are you in court today?"

"For being nosey," said the disgruntled man.

His neighbors, he explained, were having a major brawl late the night before, so he crept over to the property line and peeked through the bush-covered fence to see what was going on.

While standing there, the unlucky voyeur felt a hand on his shoulder. The police had arrived for a "disturbing the peace" complaint and possible domestic assault when they spotted the nosey neighbor on their way to the disturbance and "collared" him.

The fighting neighbors had quickly piped down and, since it hadn't escalated to violence, were just given a warning by the officers. Unfortunately, when the smoke all cleared away, it was discovered that the nosey neighbor had an outstanding warrant and the police took Mr. Jones off to jail.

"Your Honor," said the defendant, "from now on, I don't care if my neighbors wash elephants in the front yard!

"I'm minding my own business!"

Another person shocked to find themselves afoul of the law was a tiny, elderly woman who was minding her own business inside her own home. She was leashing her 100 pound dog to prepare for a walk when a cat ran passed her house. The dog, being duly offended by the feline trespasser, leaped straight through the screen of the front door and pulled the 90 pound lady through with him.

One block later, the poor woman managed to untangle from the leash and came to an abrupt stop. The dog continued his merry pursuit.

Finally, she pulled herself upright, scratched and bruised, only to be met by an officer of the law returning her dog—and handing her a ticket for allowing her dog to run *loose!*

Sometimes the long arm of the law also needs a little foot-work. I arraigned a well-built defendant on "fleeing and eluding police" who had been chased down by one of our "seasoned" officers after the young suspect ran from a car he had been driving. Both the young man and his vehicle were full of intoxicants.

"How old are you?" I asked.

"25."

"Work out?"

"Every day," he answered proudly.

"Run fast?"

"Judge," he puffed out his chest: "I hold high school track records—several."

"Then you ought to be ashamed of yourself. Do you know who chased you down?"

"No, sir."

"Officer Brock. He's much older than you. He's slower, overweight, eats junk food, and never works out. In fact, he runs faster backwards than he does forward."

The young man dropped his head in shame.

"Keep up this lifestyle, young man, and my 85-year-old mother will be able to chase you down…if you don't kill your-self first."

(I think this exchange hurt the young man more than the sentence he received).

[An aside from Karen: A great factor in John's life was his mother, Esther Doris (Laflen) Conover. She lived aggressively until her 92nd year and was a force to be reckoned with. She grew up in Collison, Illinois, a tiny farm community where she was loved and treasured by her family. Her childhood was crystallized and compressed into her favorite story about which she often reminisced and frequently retold with relish. Writ large, it captures a bygone era, and everlasting values. I repeat it here, with typical grandchildren responses in parenthesis.]

D oris Conover's story took place just before Christmas in the year 1930. A terrible thing called The Depression was everywhere. Men couldn't get work to feed their families. Women tore up old clothes and made "new" clothes out of them.

("Why didn't they just go to Walmart, *Grandma?")*

Many people were hungry and men would walk the country roads to the farmhouses to beg for a few hours of work and a small sack of food. The farmers always found something for them to do and gave them a hot plate of food to eat out on the back steps.

Grandma Doris was thirteen that Depression winter out on the farm in Southern Illinois. The farm was twenty miles from the nearest town and the road to town was narrow and rutted and one-wagon wide. If you encountered someone going the other way with their horse-drawn equipment or a newfangled automobile, you had to find a wide spot near a tree and pull the horse off the road to let them pass.

("Why didn't they just put cement on the road, Grandma?")

But it was December and the miles of flat farmland were

deep in snow. Occasional visits between isolated farms had pretty much stopped because the snow was really deep and the snow storms seemed endless. (At this point, Grandma swore that winters "back then" were *much* worse than now!)

As Christmas got closer that year, Doris and her little sister, Naomi, became worried because it seemed like their father became sadder and sadder. They were used to their father being sad a lot since their mother had died, but he seemed even worse as the holidays got nearer.

"Don't be surprised," he said to Doris many times, "if Santa can't come this year because of the deep snow and this terrible Depression." Of course Doris was way too old to believe in Santa but she hadn't told her father. He didn't say anything to little Naomi because she was too young to understand. But even she knew that Christmas might not be happy for them.

("Couldn't Santa just fly to your house, Grandma?")

Finally, two days before Christmas, the storms stopped and the sun came out on a fairy-tale land of white. Everything glistened. When Doris took the chamber pots to the outhouse to empty them *("Yuuuuuck, Grandma!!")*, the snow crunched in the bright, cold air. As Doris stood near the porch, she heard the sound of bells and looked up the road to see her grandfather coming from his farm with a small sleigh pulled by one of his strong work horses. The deep snow would have been too much for the "buggy" horses. (If we weren't careful, this is the spot where the kids would ask a million questions about horses!)

All afternoon Doris' dad and grandfather worked in the barn, except when they came in to eat. She tried to listen to their conversation at the table, but she couldn't figure out what they were doing in the barn. In those days, it was considered rude for children to ask adults a lot of questions. (This is when Grandma would look pointedly around the room at her grandchildren....)

The next day was Christmas Eve Day. Both of Doris' grandparents came down the road very early, but her father didn't stay to visit. Instead, he went to the barn and soon came out with a big covered wagon that had been outfitted with snow runners and was pulled by two big farm horses (by now the kids would be listening open-mouthed).

Without a word of explanation, Doris' father waved goodbye to her and her sister and drove off slowly down the snow-buried road, his lantern beside him on the seat.

Doris' father did not return that whole day. At nightfall, the snow began again in big, lazy flakes. When she and her sister were tucked into bed by their grandmother, each of them said a special prayer for their father's safe return. Even her grandmother looked worried and Doris began to think that maybe her father would "go away" like her mother had done and never come back.

The next morning, Doris and her little sister were up early. They were greeted happily by their father and their grandparents. The little Christmas tree in the "company" dining room had several packages under it and the girls were urged to open the presents "that Santa had brought."

Doris' sister got a beautiful doll: the first "store-bought" one she had ever owned. Doris got a red coat with a "real" fur collar which was (the kids said in

Doris and her little sister Naomi with their grandfather, John Laflen, about the time they lost their mother (and John Laflen's daughter)

unison: *"the most beautiful coat you have ever seen in your life!"*) It was a very happy Christmas for two little farm girls, miles from town, who still missed their mother.

Years later, Grandma learned the full story about that Christmas Eve when her father, in order to buy the Christmas presents, had driven a wagon-load of corn twenty miles to Danville and sold it at the grain elevator. She learned of the dangerous trip home on the dark, snowbound road and how many times her father had feared that he was lost forever, but the good farm horses had found their way home at last.

[Well, that's it. For the rest of her very long life, this story of love and sacrifice was burned into Doris' memory and heart.

Beginning in his teens, John spent many summers working on this farm and staying with his grandpa and step-grandmother (a woman of boundless love and good humor). There he learned the attitude of decency toward God, family, and community: a solid extension of what he was learning at home.

He also learned on the farm that his future did not lie anywhere near the mechanical.

One summer, John's grandfather made the mistake of sending him to Collison's grain elevator (which didn't yet exist in 1930) with a load of wheat. He instantly became a knee-slapping legend in the community for getting that wagon stuck SIDEWAYS in the grain elevator door!]

The long arm of the law is often not quite long enough!
Suspicious Fed Ex packages arriving at our local airport are often examined by trained drug-sniffing dogs. If a package is "hit on" by the dog as possibly containing narcotics or other illegal items, I receive a telephone call requesting a search warrant to open the package.

On a Sunday afternoon, I authorized such a warrant. The officers found the package stuffed with cocaine. The decision was made to dress up officers in Fed Ex uniforms and deliver the package to the address on the label.

When the officers arrived at the delivery home, the undercover narcotic agents were already staked out in a panel van. However, no one answered the door when the disguised officers rang the bell. After several attempts to rouse someone throughout the day, in the evening the narc agents put the package on the front steps and went back to the van and waited.

Suddenly, there was a blur of a sprinting figure, dressed in black, running full tilt toward the porch. Before the agents could react, the shadowy streak snatched up the package of cocaine like a football and disappeared into the night, never to be seen or heard from again….

S peaking of law-breakers on the run, on a busy court day a young lady was appearing before me on a criminal charge when all of a sudden she bolted and ran out of the courtroom!

The police department is right across from the court and several officers came running over in reaction to the commotion. The chase began—or at least everyone thought there was a chase.

The police ran out the door and headed downtown assuming that's where the woman had gone, and several local business owners joined in the search. It was a wild scene in our small town's business district!

Suddenly, in walked the young woman who calmly approached the podium. She sheepishly apologized for what she called "a panic attack." She said that when she had run out of the courthouse, she had jumped behind a big ever-green bush near the door and hid there for several minutes.

In the meantime, the furious search for the "escaped criminal" continued throughout our small community. There was really no way to call it off…besides I knew several shop owners who needed the exercise….

In night court, the police brought in a man charged with driving his family car on a suspended license.

"What do you do for a living?"

"I'm a long-haul truck driver."

I take pride in the fact that some pretty clever lawyers have failed to pull the wool over my eyes, so I was a bit nonplussed when an elderly lady outwitted me.

First, you should know that I *never* allow parties in a case, or their lawyers, to enter my chambers or in any way approach me privately unless both sides are represented. To do otherwise is called having "ex parte" conversations and is totally unethical, and basically unfair.

The lady in this situation came to the court's counter one day and smilingly asked if she could see her friend, the judge. When the message got back to my chambers, I looked out and recognized her as a member of our local Chamber of Commerce. I had assisted her in many community events.

Thinking she was there on some other community project, I invited her back to my chambers. We talked warmly about our families and what was "new" in town.

After niceties, I asked her the reason for her visit. At that, she opened her generous handbag and began spreading papers all over my desk. When I asked her what the papers were all about, she smiled sweetly and said: "Judge, I have a case in front of you next week, and I thought if I told you about it ahead of time, it would be easier for me to win!"

[I did cut this nice woman short at that point, but I did it gently and with much laughter...to my everlasting relief...because she passed away a few days later, before her case ever came to court].

O ther efforts to bias my judgment are more subtle. There was a case involving property damage from an automobile accident. The case was pending in Small Claims Court, and the plaintiff (the person filing the claim) had taken pictures of the front-end of his damaged vehicle, and I looked at them since he had presented them as evidence of his financial loss.

The plaintiff then asked if he could show me pictures of his *entire* car, including the sides and the back, claiming that he was very proud of his car, and even though the other sides weren't damaged, he wanted me to see them anyway. The defendant (the man being sued) did not object.

When the plaintiff presented the pictures to me, on the back bumper of his "pride and joy" was a huge "RE-ELECT JUDGE CONOVER" bumper sticker!

I walked myself into an "undue influence" situation in another case. A local resident had been a deer processor for many years and was reported to do a very good job at it. Therefore, one fall I took a deer I had killed to him for processing.

That very week, I was surprised to find the same person standing in front of me in court. He was arrested and charged by the DNR (Department of Natural Resources) with not having a meat processing license….

Oops.

When I balance out my sentencing decisions, I always try to be sensitive to the consequences to the victims. That was certainly the case when a young man appeared in front of me who, along with two of his friends, had severely vandalized a Little League Baseball complex where little kids play ball.

Because of the damages they had done, the Little League season was probably going to have to start later than normal, disappointing a lot of little kids, and inconveniencing many adult volunteers who would have to repair the damage and shoulder the cost.

The president of that Little League was present the day this young man pled guilty in my court. I had been told that the president was very disappointed because the other two vandals had already been treated with leniency by other judges and the miscreants had left the court laughing.

The Little League president's frustration with the justice system, and my own years of involvement with Little League, certainly spurred my anger and I launched into a stern and lengthy lecture to this young man about family, patriotism, responsibility to himself and his community, and finally pointing out the consequences of his thoughtless behavior on the lives of children and parents alike.

I then proceeded to sentence the chastened young man to extensive community service, including repairing the damage he had done, speaking to the Little League kids that summer, cleaning out dug-outs and preparing the ball fields for games.

At the conclusion of my sentencing, I turned to the president of the Little League and motioned for him to come forward from the back of the courtroom, asking if he wished to make any comments.

The president, looking confused, approached the podium and said: "Judge, I'm really sorry. I didn't hear a word you said. I'm hard of hearing and I forgot to wear my hearing aid."

I had the president sit in the front row and, asking for the indulgence of the courtroom spectators, I replayed my entire lecture and sentencing to the surprised defendant!

I figured the young man could use a double dose of butt-kicking anyway....

Some of the wisdom I'm accredited with is actually accidental.

A local man was charged in a domestic assault (verbal, not physical) of his wife after police had been called to his residence several times because both parties were disturbing the peace. Bouts of marriage counseling had evidently not resolved any of their problems.

When he appeared in court, I entered a no-contact order for both spouses, a legal command that the husband and wife could not have contact of any kind with each other. My fatherly advice to the man was that for the couple's sake, their children's safety and the peace of the community, they should get a divorce and move on with their lives.

The husband moved back home with his parents. The wife stayed in the marital home with the children, and the court set a future review date for the case.

When the review came up, the defendant-husband came to the court and immediately confessed to me that he had violated the no-contact order. But before I could react to this news, he quickly blurted out: "But Judge, thank you for saving my marriage!"

Skeptical, but curious, I invited the man to explain this revelation. Excitedly, he said that for years there had been little or no romance in his marriage, and that once I had issued the no-contact order, he would wait until two or three o'clock in the morning, when he was pretty sure "the Judge" wasn't going to be out on the streets. He would put on dark clothing, sneak through several backyards, and his wife would leave out a ladder leading from the porch to the upstairs bedroom. He would climb the ladder and enter the bedroom where he and his wife would behave like newlyweds. Following intimacy, he said, he and his wife talked out many of their problems for hours. Then he would climb back down again before dawn and go back to his parents' home.

"That no-contact order, Your Honor, was a great idea!"

"You're welcome, I think…."

Another defendant was looking for a way to win within the confines of the law.

A recent regulation became law which forbids hunters from putting out bait piles for deer in the fall hunting season and throughout the year. Hunters grumbled over not being allowed to put out piles of beets, carrots, or apples, and one hunter appeared before me who had succumbed to the urge to break this law.

The hunter was pretty unrepentant, and determined that he had run afoul of a pretty stupid law.

"Okay," grumbled the hunter. "No more bait piles on my property. But next year you can be sure that my apple trees will have some very late season fruit, and maybe a few carrots, hanging from strings on the trees."

That may be interpreting the definition of bait "piles" a little too literally….

Some days, court events can only be called whacky.

A woman defendant was charged with illegally deer hunting with a shotgun during bow season. A Department of Natural Resources (DNR) officer caught her in a stilted deer blind with the shotgun.

"Your honor," declared the defendant's lawyer, "My client was innocently rabbit hunting with the shotgun when she suddenly had to go to the bathroom. She remembered that there was a porta-potty in the deer blind so she climbed up there for a bathroom break."

Unbeknownst to the defendant (and her lawyer), the DNR officer had been hiding in the bushes before confronting the hunter and took a picture of the "rabbit hunter" actually aiming at a deer in the field with her shotgun poking out of the blind.

I called the defense attorney up to the bench and showed him the picture.

His exact words were: "Oh my God! We give up!"

I had to listen ad nauseum to another defense attorney proclaiming the magnificent character of his client. He droned on for many minutes as to why his client didn't deserve any jail time when it was obvious to everyone in the courtroom, including me, that he did.

Finally, I halted the lawyer's barrage of baloney and spoke directly to the defendant.

The defendant was a very big man, roughly bearded and muscles rolling. "I'm a hunter," I said, looking him right in the eye: "and you look like a man to ride the rapids with—to sit around a campfire with—a fair man. I've heard from your lawyer. Now, what do *you* think I should do to you?"

"Why Judge," he gruffly replied after clearing his throat several times and thinking for a minute: "I'd put myself away in the slammer for what I did." Then he hung his head.

His lawyer slumped dejectedly into his chair with a loud moan while the audience gave the defendant a round of applause.

I've been accused by some that I view my community through Norman Rockwell eyes: patriotic parades, summers at the lake, children and dogs playing safely on green mowed lawns, church on Sundays, long talks with Dad, Mom cooking dinner, and loving your neighbor like yourself. I guess I see no reason to abandon "old" values when they are still perfectly good.

One lovely summer day, as I took the bench I noticed a Good Humor man, in full uniform, sitting in my courtroom. As visions of King Cones and Cookies and Cream Bars began swirling

on the outskirts of my conscious thought, the case was called against the ice cream man.

A summer Grinch didn't appreciate this seller of frozen treats and he/she filed a complaint that the Good Humor truck was playing music too loud and disturbing the peace.

Though I don't usually tolerate audience participation, from the back of the courtroom I heard a voice express my exact sentiments:

"What is the world coming to, Judge? Arresting a Good Humor man! It's un-American!"

I sentenced the Good Humor man to quickly get back to his route. Some humorless grouch might find his music annoying, but there were kids anxious to hear it.

I should have sentenced him to leave me a Reece's Ice Cream Cup...Mmmmmm).

F ans of common sense are usually well disposed toward me and my court. If your common sense level hovers around that of a typical politician, my justice may leave you cold.

Two school teachers from outside my community bought a television set for $25 at a garage sale in my town. When the television didn't work, they filed a Small Claims action against the seller.

Both teachers took a full day off from work for the trial, dragging the TV set into the courtroom. Questioning revealed that they both had to arrange extensive lesson plans for substitute teachers. They both had to lose a personal vacation day or lose a day's pay to appear in court. All this for an "as is" $25 garage sale television!

Out of curiosity, I had the teachers place the television on my bench and plug it in. Sure enough, just snow appeared on the screen. After looking over the back of the TV, I had the court clerk bring me a screw driver and I attached the rabbit ears that were clipped to the back. A local TV station came in just fine. Case dismissed.

The teachers were heard to grumble on the way out of the court: "I think that judge just doesn't like out-of-towners!"

A State Trooper called me at home requesting permission for warrants to arrest three suspects: Mr. Wheat, Mr. Brown, and Mr. Jones.

I couldn't resist: "Would you like to harvest Mr. Wheat first?"

Chief Boyce was a retired Chief of Police in our community. When he was in his 90s he was still hunting, ice fishing, and snowmobiling. He was a former champion boxer and left a rich legacy of service to our community. Another activity he enjoyed in his later years was sitting through hearings in my court.

Chief had a special chair in my court and regularly sat there with a big cup of coffee. Often times, after listening to parties squabbling over minutia, especially within families, I would stop proceedings and say: "Chief, what do you think I should do with this case?"

Chief would rub his gnarled hands together and say something like: "I think those folks should walk across the street to Archie's Restaurant and have a cup of coffee together. Seems to me disputes, especially in the family, should be settled out of court."

Even parties who didn't know who the Chief was, recognized the authority of his character…and maybe his wisdom, because many took his advice, looked a bit ashamed, and left to work things out.

W hy are there Braille directions on the driver's side of a drive-through ATM machine? Duh! Judges also have their "Duh" moments.

Before each court session, I explain that if anyone has a physical disability or needs an interpreter, to please let us know and we will accommodate them.

At the end of one morning, after several hearings, there was one person still sitting alone in the courtroom staring straight ahead. I asked him what he was there for. He looked at me blankly and then gushed a string of non-English, arms flying in all directions.

He had obviously heard my offer for an interpreter, and had not understood a word of it. Zut Alors!

I'm a hands-on judge, and I particularly love the small-town parades. I'm always out in my community: talking, listening, and mingling. My wife accuses me of attending every gathering of more than five people.

I also have a very good memory for faces and names. If you've been in front of me…ever…I will probably remember you and your "record."

In court, a repeat criminal defendant and his lawyer were standing before me and I noticed the defendant was sweating profusely in a very cool room.

Fearing that the man might be ill, I called the defense lawyer to the bench and asked him what was wrong with his client.

"Well, Judge," said the attorney, "you were in the Homecoming Parade last week, walking through the crowd and shaking hands. You walked up to my client, recognized him, and called him by his name. He's scared to death that it's bad news for him when a judge can pick him out in a parade crowd…and that he is probably heading for jail!"

One of my favorite parades every year is at our county fair. It is quite a sight as it winds its way through the hot, dusty fairgrounds with the pungent smell of farm animals and funnel cakes baking in the summer sun.

I love it. I roll up my sleeves and sweat a pint of water while waving at little kids, carni workers, stray dogs, and Future Farmers of America contestants. I'm not sure that there are any voters in the crowd, but I shake everyone's hand anyway.

For many years I was usually selected to lead off the County Fair parade, until one year a local politician up for re-election asked me if I would be last. She argued that every year I've spoiled things for the rest of the participants in the parade.

"How's that?" I asked, just a little offended.

She explained with a laugh: "Some of the fair goers, including many of the carnival workers, have outstanding arrest warrants or have been in your court. When they see 'the Judge' coming, they take off, leaving very few spectators for the rest of the parade.

"And incidentally," she added: "after you go through, it takes the fair board half the night to round up someone to run the Ferris Wheel and the Tilt-a-Whirl...."

Familiarity with the judge can be a negative, like the guy in the parade crowd. Other times it might seem like a positive.

One evening, my wife and I were sitting in our living room and saw the flashing lights of a police car stopped on the busy street in front of our house. A popular spot for catching speedsters, we watched the officer walking back to his car with a clipboard, and a man sitting in the stopped car, slouched in his seat.

Our gawking was interrupted by a phone call and I found myself talking to one of the kids I had coached in Little League baseball several years before. We chatted for several minutes about the old team and what all the kids were doing these days. When I asked him how he was doing, he replied: "Well, I'm not doing very well, Judge. I've been captured by the police, and I wondered if you could tell me what I should do?"

"What? Are you in jail, Jim?" I inquired.

"I'm not in jail, Judge. I'm right in front of your house!"

Looking out the window, I saw cruiser lights still flashing and a grown-up Jim, cell phone in hand, waving to me from his car window!

"Uhhh, Jim...good to hear from you...."

The first judicial conference I ever attended actually offered the best advice I could have received as a new judge in a small town: never tick off the local barbers.

The unofficial mayor of our community and mayor pro tem are "Chuck the Barber" and his barber son, Scottie.

Chuck has cut hair for many years in the same location. He has cut hair for generations of families and the hair of most of the elected officials and police officers. The barbershop contains a history of the community with photos of local sports teams, police officers (past and present), pertinent newspaper articles, and tucked in there among the memorabilia is a nice picture of the local judge (ah hem). The shop is like stepping into past and current history. It is reminiscent of Floyd's barbershop from the old *Andy Griffin Show*.

Country music is always playing. Scottie sells eggs and butter from his farm. Lamps and appliances are repaired. Fresh turkeys are sold by Scottie on Thanksgiving.

Usually on Saturday mornings I stop by with my dog, a cup of coffee, and a newspaper, to listen to gossip and complaints about red tape and politicians. On occasion, I have to tell Chuck that a regular patron will not be around for his usual trim because I've put him in the slammer.

Oftentimes people come into the barbershop hoping Chuck and Scottie can have some influence on cases coming before me.

A particular customer came in one day when I wasn't there complaining about the terms of a probation sentence that I had imposed on him. Chuck told him to walk over to the Courthouse to talk to me about it.

The man appeared at my court clerk's counter a few minutes later and told her that he had been advised to ask the Judge to lighten the stiff probationary requirements that had been placed on him.

My clerk expressed surprise that the probation officer would second-guess the Judge after the sentencing, and she correctly surmised that no way would the Judge alter his sentence, regardless of the probation officer's advice.

"Oh no," the man replied. "The probation officer didn't say anything. I got my advice from Chuck the Barber."

Ummm, the sentence still stood, and I made it a particular point to thank Chuck for his service to the court...and to advise him not to quit his day job.

A defendant was scheduled to appear for sentencing in front of me.

In a visit to Chuck's barbershop, the defendant confidently reported on his upcoming court appearance to the whole shop. When Scottie asked if he wasn't worried about the outcome, he bragged that he intended to appear in court and "blow smoke up the Judge's [posterior]" with excuses and fabrications.

The smoke signals reached me before the defendant did. I arranged for him to be unavailable for his usual haircut from Scottie for several months.

The hands-down favorite story about me in the barbershop involves my wife, Karen.

Quite often late at night I receive a call from police officers requesting a search warrant to take a blood sample from a drunk driver, or a warrant for a drug bust or some other arrest.

About 3 o'clock one morning the phone rang. I was so soundly asleep that I didn't hear it. It was a steamy night in August and the air conditioner was blasting.

I sort of half woke up and saw a shear billowing nightgown floating toward me! I was instantly in eager anticipation as I saw my wife bend over me! As I excitedly reached for her, she handed me the telephone and said: "Wake up! There's a hardworking officer that needs an arrest warrant signed!"

When I'm not checking in with Chuck about sensible sentencing, I'm often at the restaurant across the street from the court.

At lunch one day, the waitress told me that my lunch would be delayed "because *someone* put the cook in jail." I quickly surmised who that someone was that had brought the popular local kitchen to a halt. Sad faces stared at me from every direction. I immediately called the Sheriff and arranged for work release for the cook.

TODAY!
Judge's Special!

Of course, from then on I have been somewhat suspicious of what might be lurking in my tuna on white....

I seldom second-guess our men in blue, but I've been known to second-guess a prosecutor or two.

Because he couldn't make bail, a defendant had been languishing in the county jail for thirty days awaiting trial on charges of growing marijuana and for a firearms violation. When he was brought into court for the preliminary examination, he was red-faced with anger.

The prosecutor presented a seized plant as evidence against the defendant, but admitted that the crime lab had lost the initial results and the re-tested results hadn't yet arrived.

I had the prosecutor bring one of the confiscated plants to my bench, and being a weekend "farmer," I pronounced that it looked like a squash plant to me. The court-room laughed politely at what they considered a lame joke. The defendant, however, was nodding his head furiously up and down in agreement with me.

A few days later, an embarrassed prosecutor sheepishly admitted that the lab results were back: the defendant was growing...squash. I'm not only good at recognizing vegetable plants, I'm pretty good at spotting prosecutorial fertilizer…. And about that firearms violation: the defendant had a double-barreled, legal shotgun in the corner of his kitchen. Considering the neighborhood in which he lived, I considered that a pretty sensible precaution.

Case dismissed!

[An aside from Karen about the real story of John's prowess in the garden]

My husband could be called a habitual gardener. In fact, my husband and I enable one another in this sick behavior. We truly need a ten-step withdrawal program!

In late winter the evil gardening catalogs arrive with lurid pictures of lush crops, baskets of succulent fruit and dizzying waves of robust flowers. In the flush of looking at these obviously doctored photos, we completely block out the memories of last summer's weed-infested, prodigal garden that even now sleeps menacingly under the winter snow, ready to assert its dominance over our best efforts to manage it.

Glassy-eyed, we draw out this year's garden plan on paper: cute little rows of beans, lovely little bushes of tomatoes, beets marching primly in single file, cucumbers on their own little hills, and (let's hold it down this year) just two squash plants.

Oh, what a lovely garden we draw on that crisp white paper!

Even in our drunken state of planning, we sometimes manage to recall the sight of quackgrass, pigweed, chickweed, pokeweed, and what-the-heck-is-that-thing weed, galloping unchecked among the dainty vegetable plants.

One year we doused the garden with pre-emergence weed killer one month (as per the directions) before we planted the garden. The hidden pigweed embryos smiled, gobbled down the weed killer and grew voluminously. The vegetable plants all died before Memorial Day. The second planting looked nauseous all summer.

I don't know if my husband just hates the work of pulling weeds, or he harbors a soft spot for the darn things, but at any rate he came home one year with a new gardening theory: "Weed and Water." You water the garden every day, and ignore the weeds. The vegetables will grow side-by-side with their weedy neighbors in a kind of rooty détente.

I think this idea came out of a demented diversity seminar.

"Weed and Water" produced a jungle of lushness all right! It was a very happy experiment…for the weeds! We needed a machete and a pith helmet to enter the garden that year, and if there were any vegetables that came to maturity, they must have been held hostage by the rampaging thistles. Occasionally, my husband would emerge from the foliage, triumphantly holding a scraggly pepper.

Another year, we hired teenage boys to keep the garden weeded. They began by pulling out the nearby rhubarb patch I had been nursing for ten years! And I don't even want to talk about the year we planted the zucchini that ate Tokyo…after devouring our garden for an appetizer.

Don't get me wrong. After paying for plowing, plants, seeds, fertilizer, weed killers, hoses, city water, muscle rubs, and a cultivator (that needs $100 in repairs every year), we have had some good crops where I didn't have to buy that "expensive" produce at the Farmers' Market. No, I can enjoy my own "free" vegetables! Of course, I figure (not counting the hours of sweat-filled labor) my "free" vegetables cost about $10 for every scrawny piece.

I think the serpent first lured Adam and Eve with a gardening catalog. We've been falling for that shtick ever since.

I was conducting a hearing on a major criminal case and had been in session about two hours.

The defendant was in handcuffs and leg irons and had been brought over from the jail by two deputies. He sat staring just above my head, glowering in silence. His lawyer, sitting next to him, presented evidence and haggled with the prosecutor on his client's behalf. The hearing dragged on while the defendant continued to look totally disinterested in the proceedings.

Finally the defendant began to act attentive to what was going on. Looking around and taking in the testimony, suddenly he began raising his hand and waving it around. Finally, I said: "Alright. Do you have a question?"

"Judge," he shouted out: "I've never seen this lawyer before in my life!"

The lawyer looked at him closely, then at his file. The court-appointed defense lawyer then admitted that he had never met this defendant before. When the smoke cleared away, it was discovered that the person in court was the *wrong* defendant.

It would have been helpful if the shackled man had noticed that the defendant's name used over and over for two hours wasn't his. When he became fully awake and looked at the charges in front of the lawyer, he began to wish he had kept his mouth shut since the crime he was actually charged with was much more serious than the one this lawyer had been defending.

Too late, the defendant said: "I will plead guilty to this charge if you can talk the prosecutor into dismissing the other charge."

Fat chance.

Defendant being questioned by me to clarify his story: "Judge, maybe I can *eliminate* this situation for you."

It was an *illuminating* situation when I was asked to speak to a class of graduating seniors from the University of Michigan, Ann Arbor.

As a true "green" Michigan State Spartan myself, I was somewhat reluctant to enter the "enemy" camp, but I agreed to go and speak about life after graduation.

The classroom was a very large, elevated auditorium and I arrived early to look over my audience and get a feel for the room. I also like to watch and listen to my audience as they filter in and try to get a sense of who they are and what they want to hear.

As the students began drifting in, I was amazed. Many students were wearing *pajamas!* Others were wearing reject clothing from charity houses. Most appeared to have been recently pulled away from their pillows or all-night parties. There were body piercings of all kinds: some looked like they had fallen face-first into my fishing tackle box. I saw every kind of hair color and style imaginable, though the most common style could most accurately be simply described as "combless." No male seemed to have a personal familiarity with razors (which may possibly apply to the females as well…). One student carried in a guitar—just in case, I surmised, that my speech was boring. Though most students appeared to be bored already. Various and sundry food was being slurped and munched, which continued throughout my presentation.

After taking the podium, I immediately changed my prepared introduction. "Good morning," I said. "I'm Judge Conover and I'm here from another planet…the planet called "Real World" where all of you will soon be going. And if you look and act like you do today, you may be on a direct path to hanging your diplomas in your parents' basements."

S peaking engagements are usually one of my favorite en-
deavors, so I was delighted to be asked to be the guest
speaker for the 50th Anniversary of the Lions Club. The
venue was to be at a luxurious country club.

This sounded like a prestigious assignment and I expected a
large crowd of Lions Club members: probably from across the
state…perhaps from many states.

I researched the Lions Club history and spent many hours
preparing what I considered to be a "barn burner" speech. My
wife was the unwitting victim of many rehearsals prior to the
big evening.

On the night of the event, I arrived a bit early (as is my habit
when I am the main speaker) and found the country club decked
out beautifully with gloriously festooned tables, fine china and
lovely flowers. The room was set up for about 500 people. I was
a bit surprised to note that there didn't appear to be any guests
there yet, though the wait staff ran around furiously attending to
last-minute details.

I hailed down someone who looked like he was barking orders and asked him where the podium was going to be located
so I could check out the PA system, and the best positioning in
addressing the crowd.

The man looked confused by my questions and consulted
with someone else, who consulted with someone else…who…
you get the idea. Finally, someone approached me and identified
himself as the person in charge. "Follow me," was all he said to
my requests for a podium and mic system.

I was led to a small room in the back of the country club.
The room barely held a table about the size of a ping pong
table, and surrounding it were a grand total of eight Lions and

Lionettes: the state officers of the Lions Club. The festivities-in-preparation I had passed through in the big room were for a wedding reception.

I was certainly disappointed, but I smiled bravely and gave the whole grandiose speech anyway, much to their amazement.

When I reported this entire tale to my wife, she reminded me of an old story about the country preacher who, because of a terrible blizzard, had only one parishioner show up for the Sunday sermon.

The preacher looked out at the lone farmer and plunged ahead with the service as if every pew were filled. He led the "congregation" in several songs; he prayed long and loud; he took an offering; he preached fire and brimstone. He even had an altar call.

At the end of the service, the parson rushed to the back door to greet his audience of one. The old farmer seemed less than impressed with the service, much to the preacher's disappointment. In defense, the pastor said: "Well, Sir, if you took your pickup out to feed your cows and only one came, wouldn't you feed that one cow?"

"Yup" replied the farmer stoically. "But I wouldn't dump the whole truckload on him."

I was conducting proceedings in the Flint City court one day. I was enjoying my usual brown bag lunch of peanut butter sandwiches in my chambers when in came some visitors. The court administrator brought in four people from mucky-muck headquarters in Lansing who were sent by bureaucrats to examine our court's financial proficiency and general security.

The little flock of inspectors filed in, each carrying a self-important clipboard and an imperious look. Unbeknownst to me, the box-checkers had had a rough morning. None of the security systems or panic button devices that they had checked had worked properly or according to their official standards. Frustration was beginning to wear on the little troop: red tape rules were obviously being neglected by us. Our court administrator, who was escorting the inspectors, was getting very nervous and decided that I would be her lifeline, so she paraded them into my chambers in hopes that I'd set their minds at ease and they'd send a positive report up the hierarchal ladder.

The bureaucrats declined my offer to take a seat and also declined sharing my sandwiches. My small talk drew out the fact that all four of my proficiency-seeking "guests" had driven separate cars from the same point of origin some fifty miles away. I commented on the incredible non-proficiency of that plan. They were not amused.

Finally, the pointed questioning came: "Just for starters, Judge, aren't you worried about the inept security system in this court?"

"Nope," I replied and took another bite of my lunch. "I rely on my own security system," I mumbled through a mouth full of peanut butter.

"What?!" came from the astonished flock.

At this, I reached into my open briefcase and pulled out a loaded .357 Magnum revolver which I'm permitted to have, and slammed it loudly on the desk.

The paper pushers all jumped back, mouths agape and pens flying over their clipboards as they furiously made notes and stammered out more questions. I calmly told the inspectors that I had a permit for the gun, and that, with the help of many fine officers and Mr. Magnum, I would take care of any security issues that came up in my court.

My wide-eyed court administrator quickly began herding the gasping group toward the door. "Thanks a lot" she silently mouthed in my direction as her parting shot.

"Don't bother to forward that report to me," I said to the closing door. And then I started in on my apple.

Some days I feel like I am sloshing among the shallower gene pool of humanity. I arraigned a motorist who was driving stark naked and paying inappropriate attention to his baser passions as he cavorted down the highway. A lady semi-driver took offense to this free spirit on the freeway and called 911. The good news: the police didn't have to frisk him for hidden weapons. He did, however, fail the sobriety test.

P art of my out-of-court personal security comes in the form of a young man that I work out with at a local fitness center. He's a weight lifter—about 6' 3", 300 pounds. He is often more protective than is probably necessary.

A story soon came back to me that when he was at a local fast food restaurant with his family, he overheard a man nearby loudly complaining about Judge Conover to anyone who would listen, and bragging how he would beat me up if he ever caught me in public.

My young friend stood up and lumbered to the table, towering over the man and said: "Hey! Judge Conover is my father (fingers crossed) and I don't appreciate your badmouthing him!"

The man looked up, ready to stand his ground, but then took in the full impact of a very large and riled man! The loudmouth suddenly remembered an appointment and quickly ran out of the restaurant.

My overzealous friend reached down, picked up the man's abandoned hamburger and calmly munched it as he returned to his family.

Thanks….I think.

Some security issues I've brought on myself. Contrary to most attorneys and judges, I sign court orders with a clear, very legible signature. I want a person to know exactly who put them in jail, signed their arrest warrant, consented to having their door smashed down in a legal raid, or signed an eviction notice.

One evening, my basset hound Molly chased a rabbit off our property and through the back woods. When I caught up with Molly she was playing in someone's yard with two little kids.

A door burst open and a grizzled, 250 pound, red-faced creature, unshaven and with a cigarette pack rolled up in his white t-shirt sleeve, yelled: "Looky here, Ma! That's the idiot that's kicking us out of our house!" At this point, I was sure that this guy was going to beat me up in front of my dog.

A disheveled woman came out of the small house and I decided to take the offensive: "Look, Ma" I said, "I'm not kicking you out of your house. You're kicking yourselves out by not paying your rent for months. I remember your case and the landlord has given you several breaks and extra time to make your payments. Why don't you talk to him and see if you can work this out."

Ma stopped in her tracks, thought for a moment, and said: "Albert, the man's right. Give him his dog back...and let him up."

Two men charged with murder were alleged to have walked into a nightclub carrying 9mm handguns and opened fire, killing two patrons and wounding a third.

At the hearing, the victim who had survived the shooting with a grazing wound to the head was on the stand testifying.

The witness described a dramatic scene: pitch dark outside, dark inside the club except for flashing strobe lights, and ear-pounding music throbbing through the building. The shooters burst through the doors and began firing randomly into the crowd. The injured victim testified that a shooter was only about twenty feet away from him when the gun turned on him. The courtroom sat in spellbound silence waiting for the rest of the witness's terrifying account.

"What happened then?" I prompted.

"Well, Judge," the man continued, "when I saw the flash of the gun, I actually saw the bullet coming at me, so I ducked."

"You *saw* the bullet and you *ducked*?"

"Yes, Your Honor."

"Mr. Smith," I asked after a long enough pause for everyone to close their mouths, "where do you work?"

"Louie's Car Wash," was his answer.

"Well, you definitely missed your calling." I replied. "With eyesight like that you should have been a baseball player. You would have broken Hank Aaron's homerun record in your first year...."

Another wounded witness gave an equally astounding account of his trauma during a hearing for assault with intent to do murder.

This man was a frustrated father whose daughter had an ex-boyfriend who would not take a hint and get lost. The boyfriend began harassing the entire family by constantly driving his truck past their house at all hours and honking loudly, then speeding away.

One afternoon, the boyfriend stopped in front of the house and the father ran out to confront the miscreant. The boyfriend sped away and the father began running down the dirt road, chasing the truck and yelling epitaphs. Suddenly, the truck stopped in the middle of the road, and the boyfriend took a rifle out of the truck and started shooting back at the father!

Incredibility, the man kept running *toward* the truck instead of running away or taking evasive action, and was therefore hit several times!

On the witness stand, the prosecutor asked the father why he had kept running *toward* the truck. His reply? He said he watched a lot of television about guns and thought that if you ran *toward* a shooter the bullets that hit you would pass *through* your body and were less likely to kill you....

I suggested that he give up cartoons altogether and watch CSI.

One year I kept track of the favorite beer of drunk drivers. I considered it a mindless distraction with little significance, but the story was covered by the local press. It seemed like not much of a story: Budweiser products easily won the "contest"—by about 80% or so. Miller products finished a distant second—and there was always a new, trendy beer that finished third.

A clear-colored beer named Zima hit the market and rapidly took over third place. Somehow word got out among the beer-brains that Zima did not register on a breathalyzer test given to potential drunk drivers by police officers.

It actually took a number of months to dispel this myth and for much of this time, guess what beer displaced Bud as the #1 beer of choice?

A man moved into our area from a big city with the idea of getting back to nature and "living closer to the land." An old local farmer who sold a bull to this greenhorn farmer was dragged into court by the buyer who wanted his money back.

Confused, the old farmer told me that "Herman" is a wonderfully personable bull and had been a family pet for years. Why was he being sued over a fine breeder bull like Herman?

When I turned to the greenhorn, it was obvious that a light bulb had just turned on in his head. Sheepishly he replied: "Judge, that was the toughest meat I ever ate."

Ignorance regarding domestic animals isn't confined to novice farmers. A rather dull young man sued a lady in Small Claims Court who had sold him a Husky puppy several months before.

When I asked the dog owner why he wanted his money back, he replied: "I wanted to breed the dog, Your Honor, but his *tentacles* won't come down!"

I could hear stifled snickers being swallowed all around the courtroom. "Are you sure you didn't buy a female, Mr. Blank? My wife says a woman's *tentacles* are always up."

Amidst the explosion of laughter, the man confusedly replied: "Well, I don't think so, Your Honor, but I'll check with the vet."

I dismissed the case for lack of evidence.

Early in my tenure on the bench, I learned that if I park my car in the general lot instead of in my designated parking space, my car is not only safer, I learn some interesting things.

A man was in front of me for driving on a revoked license. When I asked the defendant how he got to court, in detail he emphatically described how he had walked to court and his son would pick him up at the end of his hearing (assuming I guess that I wouldn't send him to jail).

In spite of a horrendous driving record which resulted in his license being revoked by me in the first place, the defendant pleaded for probation and promised to turn over a new leaf. I told the errant driver that, because of Paul Harvey, his son didn't need to pick him up after court…and that he was indeed going to jail.

When the crestfallen defendant looked confused, I explained: "Mr. Smith, while I was sitting in my car this morning listening to the end of Paul Harvey on the radio, I watched a red pickup squeal into the parking lot…and park next to me…and you, Sir, climbed out of the driver's seat…."

"Oh no!!" He exclaimed. "Was that *you*?"

In the wacky world of criminal behavior, the criminal justice system also makes occasional bonehead moves.

I conducted the hearings for all the defendants in Michigan's biggest Meth Lab bust. This case involved millions of dollars, cruel murders, and attempts to assassinate the one defendant who agreed to "flip" and testify against the rest of these brutal drug peddlers. The "snitch's" testimony was critical to convicting this group of thugs so it was important to keep him alive and healthy.

Despite law enforcement's careful guarding of the snitch, a murder attempt was made on his life by a hit man who disguised himself as a priest and nearly got to the flipper in our local jail. Fortunately, the metal detector and vigilant deputies foiled this attempt. That's when the authorities wisely decided to move the witness to a  "secret" location outside our county while the trials proceeded.

At the first court appearance, the snitch was brought into my court protectively surrounded by cops. I was impressed with the precautions to secure the safety of the star witness: that is, until the guy left the witness stand. Across the snitch's back I clearly read: PROPERTY OF SAGINAW COUNTY JAIL.

Criminals may be dumb, but....

A nd speaking of revealing clues attached to defendants…
A prominent local defense lawyer was giving his final argument in a murder trial, passionately defending a thuggy-looking client whose wife-beater sleeves were rolled up to his shoulders. Suddenly, the lawyer spotted the same thing on his client that I had noticed earlier in the trial: tattooed on the defendant's arm was the word "Killer."

The attorney spent the whole rest of his final argument trying to stand where he could block it from the view of the jury.

It didn't work.

A nd on the topic of thuggy-looking defendants, for years I had a wonderful clerk who saw the best in everyone: even hardened criminals. Toni was delightfully naïve and provided me with many funny (and sometimes *embarrassingly* funny) situations.

The night before my birthday, I studied my cases for the next day. Ruefully, I shared with my wife that my birthday would be a challenging one. I expected the courtroom to be filled with unrepentant serial offenders, most of whom knew that I would probably send them back to jail. I also noted that many of them had hired the most hard-nosed, combative attorneys available.

The next day, while I was in my chambers preparing to take the bench, unbeknownst to me, Toni had a birthday surprise waiting for me.

When I approached the bench, my grinning clerk gave a signal to the packed courtroom and dozens of disgruntled criminal defendants—soon to be sent to jail by me—and their battle-hardened lawyers—reluctantly scraped to their feet, and under Toni's beaming direction, grumbled through an off-key, begrudging rendition of "Happy Birthday To You."

Except for Toni, I wasn't really feeling it….

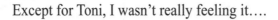

Toni's mix-ups are also legendary. We needed a language interpreter for an upcoming hearing, something that doesn't routinely happen. I asked Toni to line up a lady who had served in this capacity before: a Rose "Smith."

Toni went to our phone directory, remembered the "Rose" part of the name and called Rose "Jones"—our state representative at the time! Toni got Representative Jones' teenage daughter on the phone and said: "Tell Rose that Judge Conover wants your mother in court tomorrow at 8:30 A.M. to interpret for him."

"Wow," said the daughter. "I didn't know my mom was an interpreter!"

A little surprised by the daughter's ignorance, Toni replied: "Yes she is. Please have her here promptly on time."

The next morning, no interpreter appeared in court. Toni swore she had confirmed Rose for the job when I questioned her. Just then another clerk brought me a note: Rose Jones is on the phone from the state capitol. She wants to know why in the world she is supposed to be in your court as an interpreter!

Actual Transcript:

Judge Conover: "What excuse do you have for biting the police officer?"

Defendant: "He stuck his arm in my mouth."

Another one of the weddings I officiated was at a local pizzeria. I dragged my wife along to take pictures (and to protect me from aggressive brides!).

When we arrived, the rented room had been darkened, with only flickering candles dimly lighting the festivities. And festivities there were! The wedding party had been liberally consuming masses of pizza pies and gallons of wine well in advance of the nuptials.

With difficulty, we sifted everyone out of the dark for the ceremony, and I quickly discovered that, not only did the groom not speak a word of English, but he was also decidedly drunk.

I finally recruited an uncle out of the shadows to interpret for the groom and we all stumbled through the ceremony, with my wife blindly taking periodic flash pictures of elbows and feet.

At the end, I wasn't sure who had married whom…and I'm pretty sure the groom didn't either. I just know I had escaped without being smooched by either the bride *or* the groom.

A person who had been in front of me as a defendant several times over the years, asked me to perform his wedding and I agreed.

We were all in chambers preparing for the vows and I had started to put on my robe for the ceremony when the groom turned ashen.

"Judge," he implored, "you scare me to death in that robe. Would you please marry us without it?"

It was my court reporter Toni who called the cases for my court. Many times I fought hard to maintain my "judge face" when she innocently stumbled into a mispronunciation such as the day she was calling a case for a Mr. Bonheed. To a packed courtroom, Toni announced: "Mr. *Bonehead*, if you are here, please stand up!"

L ost items are not uncommon on busy pre-trial days. Some items are stranger than others.

On one of these days, a person came to the clerk's counter to report that there was a pair of woman's underwear on the floor in the courtroom.

The clerk rushed in to conduct an immediate investigation—then stood over the pink lacy underwear until the Chief of Police arrived.

The Chief came running into the courtroom wearing a pair of rubber gloves, and gripping evidence pinchers. He seized the abandoned panties with the pinchers and then waved them in the air above his head.

With grave authority, he barked: "Did anyone lose their underwear?"

No one answered in the stunned audience. The silence went on for several painful seconds.

Finally, breaking the awkward moment, the clerk shook her head and announced: "Obviously, Judge, you've scared the pants off another one!"

E vidently it isn't just pants that I sometimes scare off from people.

On another very busy pre-trial day someone among the court attendees brought to the clerk's counter a full hairpiece that someone had left on a seat in the courtroom.

The clerk gingerly put the hairpiece into a plastic baggie and went to the back doorway of the courtroom where she could survey the audience without being seen. She surreptitiously held up the hair trying to visually match it to a head.

She couldn't find a likely owner, and amazingly, no one, beast or human, has ever claimed that hairpiece.

One of my other happier civic duties is to give people references where it's appropriate. One young man was enlisting in the Navy but, because of several alcohol offenses on his record, he needed someone to vouch for his good character.

The young man stopped by to see me, asking if I would be his reference because, he said, considering all of the times he had appeared in front of me that I probably knew him best! We both laughed. The recruiter was shocked that a judge was being used as a reference for someone who had been sent to jail.

The truth was that he was overall a fine young man, had always totally complied with my rulings, and I thought he should have an opportunity to take his life in a positive new direction.

Happily, he went on to serve his country admirably, after finishing at the top of his recruiting class.

A local officer responded to a "theft in progress" at a video store. Upon arriving the officer met the culprit coming out of the store carrying a stack of videos and DVDs. When the officer rushed up to him, the man stopped and smiled disarmingly, then handed the officer his armful of hot merchandise as if he was giving up.

Without thinking, the officer took the stack and the thief then pushed him down and ran off.

The officer's second reaction, the correct one, was to throw the loot in the air and chase the guy down, much to the entertainment of the parking lot spectators.

A woman was charged with a felonious assault with a dangerous weapon. When I asked her what happened, she replied:

"Judge, I was peeling potatoes with a potato peeler when my drunken boyfriend tried to attack me."

"What happened then?" I inquired.

"I decided to peel him rather than the potatoes," she smiled.

"I guess," I smiled back, "everyone is lucky you weren't carving a turkey!"

A very personable and charming young woman was sadly sucked into a life of illegal drugs. As part of her probation, I assigned her to community service in addition to rehabilitation treatment.

When she had to appear again to report on her probation progress, she launched into a long citation of the volunteer work she had been doing at a local church. She had even documented her service there, listing specific days and times she had volunteered at the church's Wellness Center. I let her blather at length about her "experiences" during these service sessions, even encouraging her with questions.

"I'm very impressed." I replied. "Just let me look over this schedule a little closer...."

"Amazing!" I added as I pulled out my personal calendar. "I volunteer at the *very same* church, working on the *very same* nights, at the *very same* times that are on your service list!...and I've never seen you there, not one single time."

Hmmmm.....

I stopped wearing a watch while I was going to law school (imitating a favorite professor). However, law enforcement, lawyers and their clients alike soon learn (or get burned) from my strict punctuality. When I set a hearing or court procedure for a certain time, you can be assured that it will start as scheduled.

When a lawyer didn't show up on time to fight a speeding ticket for his client, one of my clerks brought me an urgent phone message: the attorney was stopped along the expressway...waiting for a cop to finish writing him a speeding ticket.

A high school in our area was playing in a state finals football game. The week before the big game, a star player on the team was arrested and charged with a series of felony home invasions.

Despite the seriousness of the charges, and overwhelming evidence against this young man, the school was insistent that the player should be allowed to participate in the game since it would take place "before his actual conviction." The possibility of winning a state championship was obviously more important to these "educators" than building character in athletes.

As the story spread throughout the community, many were outraged at the cavalier attitude of this school's administrative decisions, but a handful of "big wigs" were prepared to post whatever bond I set on the young man and free him to play the 7 P.M. game. I was ethics-bound to set a fair bond, but opposed to the bad message being sent to the young man: football stars play by different rules.

I solved the problem by setting a 5 P.M. to 7 A.M. home curfew as a condition of bond, so even though he was "sprung" on bail, there was no springing for goal lines in his immediate future.

I was assigned a case involving four defendants charged with several felony counts carrying many years in prison if convicted on the meth amphetamine charges.

These were tough guys—the leaders of several large motorcycle gangs. Amazingly, humor sometimes finds its way into these grim proceedings that took place over several days.

During one day's hearings, one of the court-appointed defense attorneys fell asleep at the counsel table. His client was the last type of defendant you would want to fall asleep on. I saw the defendant ask for a pen and piece of paper from another attorney. He wrote a note and the other attorney asked to approach the bench, which I allowed.

Rather than waking his attorney himself, the savvy defendant probably was setting up an "inadequate defense" appeal. The note said: "My attorneys asseep would you pleaz wake him up."

I held up my hand to quiet the courtroom, and loudly addressed the defense attorney. Three times I repeated his name before he jerked awake, sprang to his feet in obvious disorientation, and fell face first onto the counsel table as he attempted to lunge forward.

(I hope the bruises he sustained were the only ones he suffered at his defendant's hand).

Ohne of the defense attorneys in the meth amphetamine hearings also represented another defendant arising out of the same case but whose trial was scheduled after the four current defendants. In fact, this other defendant was scheduled to testify the next day against the current defendants: his former cronies in crime.

The attorney's pager went off during our proceedings and he asked for a short break. He came back to the court ashen-faced and approached the bench along with all the other attorneys and prosecutors. His client had been shot to death before he could testify against his "friends."

The prosecutor lost a great witness. The representing defense attorney lost a big fat fee. And the sleepy defense attorney from my last story didn't sleep so well after this unhappy turn of events....

In the same meth amphetamine trial, during one of the breaks, one of the defense attorneys brought in a bag of candy and began handing out pieces to all the attorneys, deputies, and defendants.

The defendants, who had spent several months in jail awaiting trial, went wild for the candy. I didn't realize that the jail has a total ban on candy for fear that someone might be diabetic and suffer some medical condition for which the county would be held responsible. And heaven forbid that a prisoner might get a tooth cavity!

After a few happy munches on the candy, the deputies suddenly remembered the "no candy" ban on prisoners, and sprang into action trying to pull globs of candy out of the defendants' mouths while they madly stuffed and swallowed.

It was a head-scratching moment for my court reporter and me. The justice system was preparing to send these brutal guys away for the rest of their lives, but we jump to defend them from the evils of candy....

An older lady was a victim of a purse snatching and was testifying in my court. After describing her disturbing experience, the prosecutor asked her if the perpetrator was present in the courtroom, and could she identify him.

The victim took her much-needed glasses out of her purse and began to squint around the room.

Suddenly, the defendant helpfully jumped to his feet and said: "Here I am!"

"Why yes, that's him!" shouted the victim.

The defense attorney just moaned....

Our local Catholic priest, Father Andrew, is one of the most influential people in our small community. He is a legend when it comes to helping others, even though the vast majority of his good deeds are never publicly known. He is greatly loved in, and outside, his church.

Even though I am not Catholic, and actually attend a protestant church a few miles away, Father Andrew and I have become great friends. As a district judge, I'm in a unique position of knowing about the severe needs of many people, so Father Andrew and I have worked together behind the scenes of our community to give help, financial and otherwise, where we can.

I also spend a lot of time volunteering at the very popular Wellness Center at Father Andrew's church, attend services there occasionally, and most people in the community assume I'm Catholic—including the elderly Bishop for our area. Whenever the good Bishop sees me at a local event, he always greets me with a big smile and says: "How's my favorite Irish Catholic judge?" Knowing that I have a sense of humor, he always assumes I am teasing him when I deny being Catholic.

At annual functions, I am often seated next to the Bishop and we are introduced together. At the last social event, there I was next to the Bishop and Father Andrew was stuck at the back of the dining room. Just like the humble servant that he is, Father Andrew smiled in amusement, and later whispered in my ear: "Judge, I bet I'm the only person in this room who knows you're not Catholic. You're sitting with the Bishop, and I'm sitting in the back…. Let me give you my confession hours, my Son."

I looked up one late fall day, just before Thanksgiving, to find a sheepish school superintendent from another county standing in front of me on a "fleeing and eluding" charge. He turned red from embarrassment as the Conservation Officer explained that she had spotted this culprit, car parked along a country road, sneaking through a cornfield, gunny sack in hand.

The hyper-diligent officer took off after the startled superintendent, who in turn started running through the cornfield, business suit and all. Ms. Conservation won the footrace and tackled him in a pile of mud, and came up triumphant with five ears of corn in the suspicious gunny sack.

Upon questioning, the Superintendent claimed that on his normal commute, he had stopped by the cornfield to get a few ears of corn for the squirrels who came to his bird feeder.

I patiently explained to the officer the chink in her legal analysis: a "fleeing and eluding" charge requires that the offender be fleeing in an automobile. Furthermore, the farmer wasn't complaining about the missing corn.

The muddied (and chastened) superintendent slunk gratefully out of the court, and the officer returned to her post guarding the county's produce fields from pilfering squirrel lovers.

Chief Brandon and his officers were dealing on a regular basis with a husband and wife who were constantly fighting and assaulting each other.

After several fruitless and frustrating trips out to the house, Chief Brandon sat the two combatants down at the kitchen table.

"How about you two get some marriage counseling?" Chief asked.

"We've done that," she said flatly. "Twice. It didn't work."

"Okay," Chief replied. "Then why don't you separate or get a divorce?"

"We'd get a divorce, but we hate lawyers. The only thing we've ever agreed on," he stated with a sideways sneer at his wife. "Besides, it's too expensive!"

"Any kids?"

"Thankfully, no," she answered with her own sneer.

"Any real estate?"

"We're renting."

"Okay, I'm going to separate you two." Chief announced.

The couple was uncertain as to whether or not the chief had such power, but Bill explained that the Captain of a ship can marry people and that the Chief of Police can separate people.

"Both of you put your right hand on my star," Bill directed. "Now, do each of you swear that you want to separate?"

When they eagerly responded that they did, he added: "Now both of you sign this piece of paper and I'll show it to the Judge."

The wife yelled: "Whoopie!" and moved out that night and headed back to Tennessee and was never seen again in our community.

They later quietly did a "do-it-yourself" divorce, which I sincerely hope was more legal than their "separation"!

A defense attorney was representing a man charged with first degree murder. He also had a charge of fishing without a license. The attorney, hoping to strike a humorous chord and soften up the damning evidence against his client, offered to plead him guilty to one of the charges if I would dismiss the other.

"You have a deal, Counselor." I replied with equal seriousness: "But I get to pick which is which."

S ubtlety is not often a strong suit of people with a criminal intent.

"What were you thinking?" certainly applied one busy Monday morning at our Flint Central Court. A long line had formed at the entrance metal detector and twisted down the street. Many people were slowly making their way through the mandatory check-point, but everyone seemed oblivious to a man holding a full-size ax and patiently shuffling along with the crowd.

The deputy working the metal detector certainly didn't need the machine to spot this violation. When asked about the ax, the man belligerently replied that he was going into court to "kill the judge."

I'm grateful that this loon wasn't fond of reading books about covert operations....

D uck hunters are required to put a wooden plug in the chamber of their shotguns to limit the guns to only shoot three times. The idea is to prohibit the overkilling of the ducks.

A man was before me charged with duck hunting without a plug in his gun. He passionately protested that the rule should not apply to him.

"And just why," I asked the errant hunter, "do you think you should be exempted from a law that applies to everyone else?"

"Your Honor," he argued, "anyone who has ever duck hunted with me can tell you that I can *never* hit those darn ducks! Everyone agrees that I have to shoot twice as many times to bag half as many ducks as everyone else! That law couldn't have meant *me*!"

S ome law-breakers just have to double-down on stupid.

A defendant stole a vehicle and then led police officers on a long high-speed chase through several townships, endangering many police officers and innocent citizens along the way.

After police drove the fleeing criminal off the road, they hand-cuffed the defiant driver and started to read him his rights: "You have the right to remain silent…." The driver interrupted the officer and growled:

"Officer, *you* have the right to shut the F__ up!"

I don't object to a defendant representing him/herself, but it has resulted in some strange court filings.

Oftentimes a defendant will request a change of "Venue," meaning that he's requesting that his trial be moved to a different jurisdiction. The idea is that the defendant thinks he can't get a fair trial in the area where the crime was committed because of pretrial publicity.

With this idea in mind, a self-representing defendant filed a motion for a change of "Menu."

There is little doubt that people are often overly influenced by the popular culture. And some of the ideas fostered by the entertainment industry aren't nearly as "cute" in real life as they are in our imaginations.

There is a famous country song sung by Johnny Cash called *A Boy Named Sue*. This macho tune, often sung to audiences in prisons accompanied by ear-splitting guitar licks, showcased the imaginary romance of rebellion, belligerence, and settling things with your fists. The allegory of the song features a man whose father named him "Sue" so that he would be picked on and bullied all his life, and therefore learn to fight back and be "tough."

In a sad imitation of this misguided life message, a man appeared in my court on an assault charge. A brief examination of his criminal record showed a long history of general turmoil and assaultive behavior. Fights seemed to find him wherever he went. His first name? "Hardtimes"—given to him, he reported, by his father, a Johnny Cash fan, in an attempt to prepare him for the hard knocks of life.

"Hardtimes," I addressed him. "Johnny Cash forgot to tell you and Sue that there's an office right down the hall in the courthouse where you can legally change your name. I suggest you consider doing that… right after you serve my sentence."

"How about 'Christian'?"

It's a thought…twang!

Some people trip themselves up with strange personal habits.

A police officer passed a motorcycle and heard the rider singing "Your Cheating Heart," off- key, at the top of his lungs.

The police officer thought this behavior merited investigation so he pulled him over and discovered that the serenading cyclist was drunk.

In jail hours later, long after the cyclist had sobered up, he was heard singing a bluesy gospel song: at the top of his lungs…and completely off-key.

An officer arrived at an after-hours break-in at a party store. As she arrived, she spotted a man running out the broken back door, arms full of stolen goodies.

The officer ran down the suspect and struggled to get him cuffed and under control, but the culprit fought viciously to escape his captor. With one hand clutching the suspect, the officer pulled out her taser gun…and promptly tased herself.

The robber quickly picked up his spoils and ran off.

The thief was eventually captured and prosecuted, but the officer had to face weeks of teasing from her co-workers who suggested that she might find it easier to "collar" a suspect if she tased the suspect instead of herself.

A man, whose young dog was constantly escaping his yard, was charged with allowing the dog to run loose. Having had a few dogs in my life who had a Houdini instinct for finding ways to run the neighborhood in search of adventure, I instructed the man to come up with a remedy to control Rex so that Rex would not run out of the owner's yard.

At his next hearing, the man brought in a picture of a very sad, but resigned looking Rex. The dog was wearing a large, secure looking collar, attached to a sturdy chain…and attached to the other end was a bowling ball.

When I asked the man if he thought this would solve the problem, or should I impose any additional fine as a strong reminder of the law, he replied: "Judge, *spare* me."

On the way home from late-night partying, a man struck a rabbit crossing the road. The soft-hearted man stopped and went back to find that the rabbit was badly injured, so he proceeded to perform a "mercy killing." He crisscrossed the road with his vehicle, back and forth over the poor creature until an officer arrived on the scene of the furry fatality. Unfortunately for this Good Samaritan, the officer smelled alcohol on the man's breath and arrested him after administering a breathalyzer test.

The man, in an alcohol fog, thought he was being arrested for killing off the rabbit.

"Can I help it?" he said in protesting his arrest. "I'm just an animal lover!"

Ask the rabbit about that one....

A suspicious husband got out of work early...2:00 A.M., and went home to his two-story condo to find a strange car parked in his assigned space, right in front of his home. When he tried the front door, he found it bolted so his key wouldn't work on it.

Imagination running wild, he ran to the communal pool and dragged as much patio furniture back to his yard as he could manage. He stacked it precariously on top of each other and clumsily made his way to the top of the pile, right under the patio outside his bedroom window. In testimony in my court, he said he "was inspired by Spiderman and I climbed right over that patio railing!"

His worst fears were realized when he peeked through the bedroom window and spotted his unclothed wife "entertaining" a strange man. The husband's outcries got the attention of the cavorting couple, and while the stranger was assembling himself in preparation to make a hasty exit, the husband jumped off the balcony and onto the hood of the stranger's car, leaving some impressive damage.

Not satisfied with the hood damage, the husband went for a knife in his car and stuck it into each of the stranger's tires. By this time, neighbors were hanging out of many windows and someone wisely decided to call in the local police.

Amazingly, by the time the police arrived, the two men were calmly sitting by the curb, waiting for the tow truck to arrive. The husband was nursing a sore ankle, and the stranger was fearful that his wife would get wind of the incident, so the men had worked out a deal: the interloper would forever stay away, and the deceived husband wouldn't rat on him to his wife…nor would he kill him. Also, the cheater would fix his own car. However, the police weren't "in" on the deal, and arrested the husband for "malicious destruction of property."

When the husband appeared before me, he relayed the entire sordid story, including his reconciliation with his unfaithful wife. In summary, I explained to him that I couldn't sentence him unless the victim of the smashed car would come to court and testify in person as to what damage his car had suffered.

"Oh, Judge," the man replied. "He ain't gonna show up in your court, because then his wife is gonna find out about the Booty Call that went bad…."

The what???

At the conclusion of a civil case, everyone was packing up to leave when one of the parties, a well-dressed businessman who had impressed me during the case, asked to approach the bench.

"Judge," he said, shaking my hand. "You saved my life ten years ago with a 'Bam-Bam' suit, and I never had a chance to thank you."

Well, I had to admit that I was stumped by this assertion, even though the man looked faintly familiar to me. I had to hear the rest of his story.

He went on to tell me about years of heroin addiction that began in his teenage years. During that time, the man had appeared before many judges on many charges. He claimed that the judges and counselors he was forced to see gave him probation, lectures, and a string of "second" chances. They probed his feelings, his family history, and his psyche...barely interrupting his life of drug abuse.

"Then," he went on: "I came in front of you, Judge, on still another drug charge. You sent me straight to jail for one year, and when I tried to pretend I was working and needed daytime work-release from jail, you weren't buying. After years, for once I knew I wouldn't be able to get my hands on my drugs for a long stretch of time."

"How did you handle it?" I asked.

"Well, I asked the Sheriff if they had a treatment for heroin addiction in the jail. He said 'Sure,' and put me in a 'Bam-Bam' suit and locked me up."

The so-called Bam-Bam suit was like a body straitjacket and it kept him from hurting himself while he went through a cold turkey withdrawal from a body full of drugs. Under watchful eyes, he suffered tremors, chills, cramps, hallucinations, and sometimes worse, but he came out alive and clean.

"Judge," he continued, "I went through absolute hell and when I came out of jail, I never touched drugs or even alcohol from that day to this one. It was rough, but it saved my life. Thanks."

Fortunately for this man, a swift kick in the Bam-Bam was worth several kisses on the checks from well-meaning officials.

A man was charged with destroying plant life when he drove his car through a garden at a local park. A witty lawyer who was in the audience waiting for his case to be heard, ran into my court reporter's office, grabbed a plant off her desk, ran back into the court to stand next to the Defendant and addressed the court: "Your Honor, I'm here to represent the victims in this case...."

[An aside from Karen: the public fear of the misuse of plants such as marijuana are well-founded. And certainly, John has seen the legal issues in this regard. However, I just want to warn you about an insidious plant whose dangers are not so well known. Therefore:]

This is a public service announcement:

I don't mean to scare you, but the truth is simply not getting out there. Morning Glories are unabashed killers! I'm not kidding! Morning Glories eat everything in their path: docile domestic plants, outlaw weeds which were thought (especially by gardeners) to be indestructible, chipmunks, and small children!

Okay, I may be exaggerating a bit.

But this is serious! Morning Glories are not your friends, and they are definitely not glorious! And the deceit starts at the seed store. Yes, people actually, on purpose, buy these darn things and purposely, deliberately plant them within reach of their home and loved ones!

Morning Glories look so innocent in the package! Cute pictures of little blue climbing flowers dance across the seed packets, inspiring daydreams of barefoot romps through fields of waving posies. The package says they are "hearty." Ha! Panzer tanks are hearty! Mosquitoes are hearty! Morning Glories are Genghis Khan with nine lives!

What the package doesn't tell you about Morning Glories (and this is where the public service announcement comes in) is that they are the sharks of the plant kingdom. Oh sure, you expect weeds to be uncivil little monsters. You expect to spend a fortune and the health of your back trying to kill that myriad of weeds that are too rude to die, and who will eat all your wimpy perennials in the time it takes you to unkink the non-kink hose. What you don't expect is that Morning Glories make pigweed look like daisies! The truth is that Morning Glories are the meanest, nastiest, most indestructible leafy carnivores in the plant kingdom!

The saga began five years ago. We planted Morning Glories

along the fence at the back of a very large, very spoiled flower garden. After a few weeks, we rushed down to the fence early in the day to see the dainty little blue flowers which are so shy they only bloom for a few minutes each morning. We didn't realize until July that the Morning Glories need their strength for the rest of the day to python-wrap their crawling/climbing tentacles around the neighboring plants and strangle them to death! By August we began pulling out Morning Glories by the bushel-full, usually losing the victim-plants in the process.

It was a race: us strangling Morning Glories/Morning Glories strangling our flower gardens (with their evil little blue eyes on nearby cornfields!) We focused like a pincer division on those rotten plants and pulled them out in frenzied fits. Though we were bruised and exhausted, we thought we were winning....

Now we know this wasn't the war; it was a skirmish and we didn't win...because each June, we discover **thousands** of Morning Glory seedlings taking root in our flower beds. The darn things seed themselves! And did I tell you that baby Morning Glories have goo-goo heart-shaped leaves? There's a Sunday School lesson in there someplace!

Two weeks ago, I spent about six hours clawing Morning Glory seedlings (some the size of a pea) out of our flower beds. I determined to nip this in the bud once and for all! I worked past dark, pulling out the little vultures by feel, growling incoherent threats as I crawled amidst my terrified Bee Balm.

Did I win this round? You tell me. I sit here covered with a poison ivy rash which ambushed me in the dusk from stealth deployment near the Morning Glory seedlings. Don't' tell me this isn't a war!

Take my word for it: if there are flowers in Hades, they're Morning Glories! Plant them at your own peril!

Where's the Calamine Lotion.....?

Blue-eyed Devils!

90-year-old man was charged with illegally trapping raccoons using illegal traps from the 1950s that, instead of just capturing those that wander into these traps, actually kill the animals. A Department of Natural Resources officer who confiscated the traps, and the dead animals, was in court to testify against the elderly defendant.

When I questioned the man about his traps, he claimed that he suffers from Alzheimer's and didn't even remember putting out the traps.

Not sure the old codger wasn't being cagey, I asked: "Do you remember what you were trying to catch in those traps?"

"Well, Sir," he smiled mischievously. "It wasn't supposed to be that mangy cat from the neighbors."

I looked at the DNR officer and he disgustedly nodded in the affirmative. What was left of the neighbor's cat was among the "evidence."

shoplifter ran out of a local grocery store with steaks he had stolen and stuck down his pants. In court, the prosecutor meandered around, asking a witness several irrelevant questions until I stopped him.

"Sorry, Judge," he said. "I was just trying to get to the meat of the matter."

"Fine," I replied, "but just trim the fat."

A s God as my witness, a man named Mr. Buck was charged with illegally hunting deer over a bait pile.

A man who had recently been to prison, was out on probation. But it is obvious that he didn't take advantage of turning his life around because he immediately went out and robbed a liquor store.

Along with the cash, the masked man stole a bottle of Vodka. But on the way out of the store, he tripped and fell, breaking the Vodka bottle under him and cut his leg. He then got up and ran away.

The police gathered a blood sample off the pavement, ran a DNA match and quickly identified the culprit. They arrested him while he was enjoying his last cocktail at a local bar.

Prisons may seriously need to consider providing courses in Logic…especially since the Sunday School classes in Ethics didn't take with this guy.

S peaking of party stores, an officer arrived at one where an armed robbery was in progress. The policeman had his gun drawn in anticipation, but he didn't expect a young woman to run out of the store—topless— wearing only a thong!

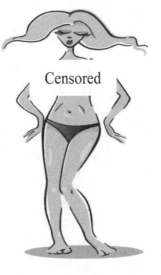

Censored

The officer took in every detail of the sight—but missed the gun she was holding, and she opened fire on the gawking lawman. Fortunately, the thief's aim must have been thrown off by the reverberations of her jiggling body parts, because her wild shooting gave him time to take cover.

Lady Godiva didn't get far. Her get-away driver had chickened out and left her behind, and as the Michigan evening grew frosty, she was found nearby shivering underneath some pine scrub.

The thong thing? Who knows what thinking went into this strategy, but it gives a new meaning to being caught red…ah… handed.

A woman appeared before me who was caught shoplifting cat food for the second time. "Your Honor," her lawyer said: "My client has some major psychological issues. In fact, she doesn't even own a cat!"

"This is a real head-scratcher," I replied. "Maybe she thinks she *is* a cat."

I've had many a double-take in court, but this one sure caught me by surprise:

Many lakes have a "Slow Wake Zone" to protect other boaters and swimmers. A defendant appeared before me who was charged with violating this ordinance on a local lake. The only problem was: the defendant was *rowing* his boat!

Michigan's No-Baiting law for deer has been a subject of great contention among hunters and the Department of Natural Resources. However, much to the disgruntlement of hunters, some DNR officers have taken enforcement of this law to an extreme.

A hunter spent an afternoon in a tree blind, eating apples and tossing the cores to the ground. When a DNR officer checked on him and found the apple cores on the ground, he arrested the hunter and charged him with, you guessed it, baiting deer!

Since I carefully review cases before they appear in front of me, I can anticipate when there's a strong chance that I will be remanding a defendant to jail time.

While hearing a relatively minor case on a fishing violation, I glanced down at my docket and determined that in an upcoming case, with a defendant still waiting in the audience for his turn, that a trip to jail was highly likely for him. As is my standard procedure, I quietly passed a note to my court reporter asking her to have a deputy sheriff come into the court to be ready to take custody of that defendant when his case came up.

For whatever reason, the deputies in the holding area

mistook her message for an emergency situation. All of a sudden, deputies with weapons drawn began bursting through the doorways and surrounded the poor defendant who had dared to fish without a license!

When the crisis was sorted out and the color was finally returning to the fisherman's face, I decided that he had been punished enough and probably would not re-offend.

I hear that that fisherman eagerly warns all his fishing friends to keep their fishing licenses current. He holds court at the local hardware: "Don't mess with that judge!"

The first time I ran for judge (unsuccessfully!), my children were very young. Perhaps the campaign, which was pretty grueling, got a bit too aggressive and this wasn't lost on my young son.

While putting up political signs in one neighborhood, my four-year-old son ran into an adjacent yard, pulled down his pants and peed all over my opponent's sign. When I yelled at him, he yelled back: "It's okay, Dad. I took care of this one!"

Vote for
FRED

One section of my voting district is well known as a no-nonsense, working class community. It was settled several decades ago by great numbers of inflowing Southerners when Flint, Michigan was the center of the auto industry. Many of these simple, honest factory workers have proudly kept their rural roots and have been some of my best friends over the years.

While collecting petition signatures to run for my judicial position, I went door-to-door in those neighborhoods with a friend from that neighborhood. I was standing next to a garage getting a signature from a man who was (illegally) raising chickens within the city limits.

Suddenly, a huge rooster jumped off the roof and landed on my head, flapping wildly, with a death grip on my scalp. While the owner stood watching with amusement, my friend batted at the critter but only made things worse. Finally, I did a somersault in the yard to dislodge the cranky rooster and came up with little of my dignity left and several peck marks on my head and on my petition papers.

The chicken raiser smiled: "That's why I don't need no guard dog," he said. Then he laughed uproariously as he signed my petition.

While collecting petition signatures in the same neighborhood on a very hot summer day, my friend and I knocked on the door of someone my friend knew.

We heard a holler from the backyard in response to our knocking, and we walked around the house to be greeted by a woman sunbathing on her stomach.

When my friend called out and identified himself, she smiled and stood up, leaving her bathing suit top lying on the ground. Without batting an eye, she strolled over and signed my petition and wished me well in my campaign. We made a quick and nervous exit.

As we made our way to the next house, my friend stopped and grabbed my arm: "John," he said, "*Anytime* you need help going door-to-door, I want you to call me!"

A young man was fishing with his small son at a local lake. When a Department of Natural Resources officer checked his bucket of fish, he found it full of catfish which were perfectly legal to catch. However, near the bottom of the bucket, he found a small bass which was not legal to catch.

The officer said: "This bass is out-of-season and it's too small even if it was in season. Why didn't you throw it back?"

The man admitted to knowing it was illegal to keep. "But," the young father argued, "this is the first fish my son has ever caught on his own. He's only three years old. He just wouldn't be able to understand why he couldn't keep it and show it to his mommy."

The DNR officer issued an appearance ticket to the man, and then took possession of the bass which he photographed, weighed at a nearby meat market, and disposed of it in a DNR approved trash receptacle.

When the two hardened criminals, father and son, appeared in my court, I fined the father $10. I then showed his son all the mounted fish and animals decorating my chambers and gave him a few fishing tips, including admonitions about only keeping fish that are big enough to leave their mother.

WANTED!
Bass Bandit

Anew young lawyer appeared in front of me on a major criminal case. He had had been court appointed to represent a man who was most likely headed to prison for many years.

The lawyer, who had not yet had many paying clients in his infant career, proudly announced that he was no longer court appointed, but that he had been hired by the family to represent the defendant.

I motioned for the lawyer to approach the bench where I quietly asked him if he had been paid any money as a retainer to represent this defendant. When he sheepishly admitted that in his excitement to get a paying client, he had forgotten to ask for a retainer, and he hadn't yet received a dime. I gently suggested that he may not ever see the defendant again after the current court proceedings. He looked stricken. I adjourned the case until later that afternoon so that the lawyer could "consult" with his client and the family.

Later, when the young lawyer's case came back to court, I again had him approach the bench.

With a big smile, he opened his sports coat. A few bills were stuffed in his pocket.

"Proceed," I ordered.

In my early years as a judge, almost every lunch hour I walked downtown in our small community to visit the local stores. I never get enough of shaking hands and meeting my fellow citizens.

One hot summer day, I wandered into a local clothing store that was always over-crammed with clothing racks. At the back of the store I spotted a woman, a long-time friend and local teacher.

I snuck through the store and came up behind my friend as she was looking through the clothes rack. I stuck my finger in her back and said: "Stick 'em up."

The woman shrieked, jumped in the air and, to my dismay, turned out to be someone I had never seen before in my life! I apologized profusely, trying to explain that I was really the harmless local judge, and backed out of the store, leaving the manager choking in laughter. I could still hear the woman's outraged cries as I hustled down the street.

The store owner enjoyed telling this story for years, describing it as my first re-election effort at soliciting votes.

A young man was standing in front of me on a relatively minor alcohol-related offence. He wasn't paying a lot of attention to what I was saying, and didn't seem to be taking his situation very seriously. His parents looked dismayed at his disrespectful behavior. Outside the courtroom there was the sound of hammers from maintenance working on something in the building.

"Do you know what that noise is, Son?" I finally asked.

"No," he answered with little interest and a lot of attitude.

"Well, once a month I pick one person to set an example to the young people in the community. The sounds you hear are workmen building a stock, you know that thing from your history books that you stick your head, hands, and feet through, and people come by to see your punishment and little kids throw rotten fruit at you. We gather girl scouts, boy scouts, and other young people to show them what happens when they don't follow the law—and to remind them to listen to their parents, do their homework, stay away from bad friends, to follow the rules and show respect to others.

"I think you, young man, are the perfect candidate for this month's example in the stocks."

It was obvious to most everyone that I was kidding, but the young man, uncertain of my real intentions, went from sulky indifference to full atten-  tion. When he looked to his parents, they pretended to accept this idea.

When I laid out his terms of probation, the young man took in every word and eagerly agreed to comply with every point, frequently glancing nervously toward the hall.

"On second thought," I wrapped up: "I may have been wrong about you being this month's pick for the stocks. I'll see you next month to review your progress and to ask your parents for an update on your behavior."

I'm happy to say that he met all his probation requirements and he never again appeared before me as a defendant.... I'm *unhappy* to say that I never could get permission for that stock thing: darn.

National politicians give lots of lip service to patriotism (mysteriously enhanced by impending re-election), but small town America is unabashedly patriotic. Marching veterans in summer parades are not props for some candidate's resume. Kids wave American flags, adults take off their hats, and some ladies cry when the old soldiers march by.

When I have the fun of participating in a local parade, I usually walk the parade in front of a truck carrying many flags representing the surrounding communities, and of course the American flag.

When we decorate the parade truck, there always seems to be disagreement as to which side of the truck the American flag should fly. It's not unusual, in the middle of the parade, for veterans from the local VFW post to begin yelling at my truck driver that the flag is on the wrong side. Sometimes they even run out into traffic, stop the parade and jump on the back of the truck, grab the flag, and switch sides.

I always thank the guys profusely and apologize for the error. Nevermind that, parade to parade, the "official" side seems to change. Maybe it depends on which direction the parade is going? I'm never sure, but I am sure that you *don't argue with a veteran*!

I'm on their side.

S trange "hiccups" haven't just occurred during my election campaigns. On an Election Day itself I rented an airplane with a trailing banner that said: "Elect John Conover— District Judge."

I spent most of Election Day scouring the skies, looking for my extravagant investment, and cursing that I had pre-paid the pilot for a service that was not showing up.

Unfortunately, the pilot confused me with a sitting district judge from a bordering county whose name closely resembles mine and he spent all day flying over the wrong election sites, in the wrong county!

In the late afternoon, the neighboring judge called me up, laughing: "Conover," he said, "did you lose an airplane or are you trying to take *my* job?"

The good news: the pilot flew around for hours and hit every polling place. I guess you already know the bad news....

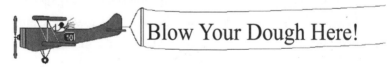

Blow Your Dough Here!

The Sheriff and I took a page from the errant pilot who flew my campaign banner in the wrong county. We were doing joint campaigning and making a point of hitting every summer parade we could find. It soon became dizzying, running from small town to small town: like chasing rabbits. The parades soon became indistinguishable from each other.

We arrived at one of the parades together with our huge flat-bed trailer pulled by a big truck. We had people passing out literature. We had kids with balloons. The trailer blared patriotic music and was covered with lots of flags, and draped with red, white, and blue bunting.

About halfway through the parade route, people began yelling at us. I finally understood what they were saying: basically "You guys are campaigning in Shiawassee County!" totally outside our voting districts....

P arades also include some "what are you thinking?" moments. I've done many parades each year, for many years. Regardless of where the parade venue is, somewhere along the route the same woman jumps out from behind a tree or vehicle, smiles, and takes my picture. She then gives me a thumbs-up, and runs off before I can hail her down.

I do not know who this woman is, and I have never seen any of her pictures.

Hummmmm....maybe I should check the target pictures at the local firing range.

A ll the municipalities that I serve have deep-seated community pride. And because they tend to be small communities, they aren't fooled by election-year pandering when candidates show up for local parades spewing candy and handshakes.

The Fall Homecoming Parades are the really big things in small towns and are enthusiastically attended. They also draw political candidates like possums to bait piles.

Because I'm such a parade enthusiast, I show up to walk in every parade in my jurisdiction, every year, whether I'm on a ballot or not.

One fall evening, weeks before a large political election, I showed up at a Homecoming Parade with my usual float and flair. Several politicians had already arrived with their "people" and floats: politicians who hadn't been seen in public since their last election.

The parade circled around the main streets of the small community, and headed for the football field where we would follow the high school band, and the Homecoming "queens" onto the field and be cheered by the packed stands.

As we approached the entrance to the football field, the superintendent of the schools called a halt and announced that my float was the only political float that would be allowed to continue, because I was the only elected official who showed any interest in their community when I didn't need their votes.

There's a life lesson in there somewhere.

I was walking a parade on a hot July afternoon. It was so hot the crowd was hanging back from the blistering curbs and taking shelter under any scant shade. My wife and kids were driving the parade in our festooned car while I ran alongside shaking hands and waving to friends. I was years away from re-election, but I just couldn't pass up a parade!

I jogged up into a yard where several people were sitting in lawn chairs drinking beer. I reached down to shake hands with a bearded guy in a floppy hat who appeared to have a cheek stuffed with chewing tobacco.

I greeted him as usual: "Hi, I'm Judge Conover. How 'ya doing?"

He grabbed my hand, pulled me down on top of him, and growled directly into my face: "I know who you are—you put me away!"

Thinking this guy was going to beat me up in front of my kids and friends, I blustered back: "Did you deserve it?"

He thankfully let go of my hand so I could regain my footing and with a mighty laugh said: "You know, I never thought about it...but I guess I did! Yah, I guess you were fair with me!"

He stood up, spit a stream of brown juice right next to my shoe, slapped me on my back and drove me halfway across the yard and back into the procession.

"You're OKAY! Judge" he shouted, followed by a big horse laugh.

When I first became a judge, I made an effort to meet all of the different players in the criminal justice field with whom I might have contact in my court proceedings.

I was told that a group of undercover narcotics agents had a trailer in a secret area of my jurisdiction where they conducted drug deals.

One hot summer afternoon, after all court business was concluded, I made the naïve decision to locate the clandestine trailer and "meet the guys" who might be bringing cases to the court.

As I drove into the rough area of town, the agents had no idea I was coming, and they certainly didn't know who I was. As I approached the trailer, a surprised agent, thinking I was a drug dealer blowing their cover, came running out of the trailer, hand over his concealed weapon.

He reached through my window and pulled me out of the car, yelling at me to identify myself.

I don't think I've ever talked faster in my life.

And I immediately stopped visiting people at their job sites…especially undercover ones.

Anytime I'm invited, I eagerly accept an opportunity to speak to students of every age group. I find they are fascinated with legal issues and, no matter how young they are, they ask lots of great questions.

I spoke most of the day in one school to many different groups. At the end of the day, as I was leaving, a youngster stood up, stuck his thumb in the air and said: "You're the man!"

Heady praise!

In another classroom, I was not as proud of my performance. It was in Mrs. Webb's second grade classroom (combined with the second grade class next door) and it took place several years before I became a judge.

There to speak about the "wonderful world of law," during Career Week, I began my little presentation by writing my name on the board. After a few introductory comments about how to become a lawyer and how many tedious years of school it took to become a lawyer, and how you have to pass a very tough test, called a Bar Exam, to become a lawyer, I then turned to write "LAW-YER" on the board.

Unfortunately, every time I wrote the word, it didn't look right. I wrote "LAYWER," turned to speak to the class and saw Mrs. Webb laughing behind her hand; looked back and crossed it out. Then I wrote "LAWYAR," turned to speak to the class and saw both Mrs. Webb and the next door teacher laughing; looked back and crossed it out.

I asked for help among much laughter, and by now even the teachers weren't in agreement on how to spell "LAWYER!" Even the kids made several spelling suggestions!

I finally erased the whole mess and wrote: "ATTORNEY!"

(Maybe they need to add "how to spell your profession" to the Bar Exam!) Thank goodness "JUDGE" is relatively easy!

A classroom full of elementary kids will always come up with a funny story. Very recently I spoke to a granddaughter's third grade class, again during a Career Unit. This time, of course I spoke about being a judge.

After several descriptions of what my job entails, and answering a whole lot of very good questions from the class, I hoped that the children were impressed with my efforts to squelch crime and discourage would-be criminals. I told them that our little community has the lowest robbery rate in Genesee County and called on them to tell me why. (Of course, I was fishing for a compliment on my job performance!).

One little boy was eager to answer: "It's because we have very tall trees," he proudly announced.

"Really?" I replied. "That's fascinating! How do tall trees keep us safe from robbers?"

"Well," he answered thoughtfully, "people who live in the other towns have short little trees that are really bushes. The robbers hide in the bushes until it's dark, and then go in and rob places! Our tall trees don't give them any place to hide!"

Wow! And all this time I've been thinking it was my tough sentences....

The younger the children I speak to, the more fun it is! Day Care, preschool, kindergarten: the challenge is great and the reward is greater!

My favorite activity with these little ones is to read them a very active story with lots of animals. Whenever we get to an animal, I ask the class to make the appropriate animal sound that goes with that animal. They always enthusiastically comply.

One day I had a bunch of great little kids quacking, grunting, mooing, barking, and growling…all at the same time. The teacher motioned for me to step outside the room for a minute. While we stood there, with the door firmly shut, we could hear the cacophony of animal sounds pounding on the walls as the volume increased.

"Uh, Judge," began the teacher. "I appreciate that the children are having a great time in there, but please understand that you get to leave in a few minutes and *I'm stuck with them for the rest of the school day*. Could you maybe read a calming book and bring them down from the ceiling?"

We both laughed and I promised to bring control back to the room.

When she re-entered the classroom ahead of me, the noises calmed down until a little boy said: "Uh, oh! Teacher made the judge go in the hall!"

A lawyer who is diabetic had a criminal case scheduled in my court. On the day of the hearing he was not feeling well but felt compelled to serve his client by not adjourning the case. He informed me that he needed an apple or some candy and a few minutes to recuperate.

I took him into my chambers where my home-packed lunch was waiting. Not knowing which foods would be the most helpful, I simply laid out my whole lunch plus a few spare snacks I keep on hand: an apple, a banana, a fruit bowl, a candy bar, some chips, a nutrition bar and some cookies. I told him to take his pick and rejoin us when he felt better. Then I left and returned to the bench.

Some time later, the attorney completed his hearing, thanked me and left.

The lunch break came late that day, and I eagerly returned to my chambers, stomach growling all the way. Much to my surprise!—all the food was gone!—my entire lunch and all the snacks had vanished! Empty wrappers in my basket told the sad story.

Does it pay to be a nice to a criminal defense lawyer?

(There's a joke in there somewhere…)

Police get used to domestic abuse calls, but this one took a strange new twist.

A husband and wife were having a domestic dispute (legal talk for a knock-down fight). In the kitchen, where the dispute began, the wife started throwing knives and pans at her husband. The husband made a mad dash into the dining room, wife in close pursuit, where the couple kept a huge aquarium tank with a three-foot pet lizard.

In the exchange of blows, the husband fell into the reptile tank where he found a very unamused lizard trying to mind his own business. The stepped-on lizard repaid the visitor with much slashing and biting before the man could make a hasty retreat.

"I'm assuming," I told the feuding couple when they appeared before me in court: "that the lizard made the 911 call."

A thief came into a nearby Walmart to steal a television. He grabbed it and headed for the exit. Outside the store manager chased after the culprit, grabbing onto the TV and getting into a classic tug-of-war. The manager then fell to the floor and broke his arm, but the security guard nabbed the would-be shoplifter.

The unsuccessful thief was charged with....*unarmed* robbery.

Under the category of "You're kidding, right?"

A bunch of guys were playing beach football at a local park. A "Hail Mary" pass hit a seagull flying by, knocking the bird to the ground near the group.

A park ranger who had been patrolling nearby, seemed to appear out of nowhere, yelling at the stunned men, and immediately began mouth-to-beak resuscitation on the feathered victim. Amazingly, the bird recovered and flew away.

In a fit of overzealousness, the park ranger then ticketed the astonished quarterback and charged him with cruelty to animals.

When the ball-throwing culprit appeared in front of me in court, he told me the whole story.

"Wow," I observed: "I hope that park ranger got a bird flu shot."

A woman on a repeat domestic assault case: "Your Honor, I'm tired of *drugging* him into court."

A defendant was in court charged with using a taser on his neighbor. After some questioning, I discovered that he had a fetish for tasering willing (and some unwilling) victims among his family and friends. As part of his sentence, I "revoked" his right to own tasers.

I couldn't resist: "You have a pretty shocking habit there, Son. We need to find a Taser's Anonymous for you."

One day I was following a squad car down the freeway that had a prisoner in the back seat. As I drew parallel to the police cruiser, the man turned around, looked at me, and there was instant recognition that we had met before. As I passed the squad car, the prisoner appeared to be in a state of high agitation.

An hour later, the same person appeared in front of me on an arrest warrant. I began looking over his long rap sheet, and reviewed his previous appearances in front of me.

"Judge, you're everywhere. You must be watching me like a hawk," he said dejectedly. "Are you my guardian angel?"

"No," I replied. "I'm your conscience stimulator. Your conscience seems to have stalled out somewhere along the way in your life. Let's find a sentence that will give it a jump start...."

He looked hopeful until I continued, "...just short of an electric shock."

I was filling in for another judge whose jurisdiction includes some of the poorest neighborhoods in my county. I was hearing landlord/tenant eviction cases, and there were dozens of them scheduled for that day. The courtroom was packed with landlords, tenants and many of their families. The winter day was blustery.

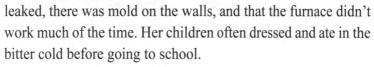

A tenant stood up and tearfully explained that she had rats in her basement, the roof leaked, there was mold on the walls, and that the furnace didn't work much of the time. Her children often dressed and ate in the bitter cold before going to school.

After a brief and pointed discussion with the landlord, I dismissed the case against the tenant for failing to pay the rent, and then chastised the landlord for failing to make this dwelling livable. I then gave him a deadline to fix the furnace, de-rat the basement, and report back to me.

The tenant who had just testified, turned to the filled courtroom, threw her arms in the air and shouted: "Hallelujah! Praise the Lord! Thanks to Judge Conover, there is justice!"

The people in the court jumped up and gave her a standing ovation to celebrate her victory, even though I'm sure they all knew it was a small victory in the scheme of their lives....

A defendant was released from Jackson Prison at 10 o'clock in the morning and given a bus ticket back to our community where he still had some family.

He was arrested in the early evening of the same day breaking into a safe at the local hardware store. He had dawdled around the store well after the security alarm went off, making it easy to catch him at the scene of the crime.

On his way back to prison, he told police that he was lonesome for his friends in jail, and wanted to be back in his "own" bed....

Gives a new meaning to "Auld Lang Syne," doesn't it?

The vast majority of criminal behavior that I see results from substance abuse and/or unleashed anger. Together, the results are catastrophic. People behave without any consideration of the pending consequences.

A woman who was distressed about some minor issue, had a few drinks and went to visit her boyfriend for comfort and sympathy—only to find a strange car in her boyfriend's driveway.

She found the door locked, and no one responded to her knocks. She started pounding on the door and yelling curses. No response. Then she heard noises coming down the stairs inside the house.

Suspecting another woman (she was right) was enjoying her boyfriend's affections, she retrieved a 9 millimeter gun from her car and opened fire on the house, shooting through walls and windows, critically striking her boyfriend.

In a blind rage, the woman then drove a block to a hardware store, bought a hammer and knife, drove back to the house and bashed in the windows of the other woman's car. When the police and ambulance arrived, she was ferociously slashing the woman's tires for good measure.

The final irony: the boyfriend had given her the gun to defend herself in emergencies.

In arraigning her: I couldn't help but comment: "Let's just say: whatever small issue began this fiasco, it's this court's opinion that your behavior failed to solve it."

"The whole thing," she agreed sadly, "was probably a bad idea."

Uh huh.

I always keep my briefcase on my desk in chambers. At the start of the day, I held a conference with the prosecutor and a defense attorney in my chambers. As we concluded, the defense attorney stood up to go into the courtroom, and accidentally picked up my briefcase thinking it was his.

A few minutes later, I put on my robe to go into the court and start the trial we had been discussing. When I reached for my briefcase, of course it was gone.

Thus began a frantic search. My court administrator walked the block to the parking ramp and checked my car. My court reporter went to the clerk's office and the probation office. An "all-points bulletin" was raised for my missing briefcase.

Meanwhile, in the court, one of the deputy sheriffs said to the attorney: "Why do you have two briefcases?" One was on the floor next to his chair, and mine was perched on the table.

In jest, I threatened the embarrassed attorney with felony theft charges.

"But Judge, I safely returned your property!"

"Ah-ha," I replied, "but where's my apple?"

At a Small Claims hearing, a woman sued for emotional distress for the loss of her small pet dog. The neighbor's pit bull ate it for lunch one day.

"I can understand your being emotionally upset," I told the woman sympathetically.

"Thank you, Your Honor," she sniffed. "But I'm not suing for *my* grief."

"You're not?" I questioned.

"No, Your Honor. I'm suing on be-half of my basset hound, Henry. They were best friends." And she burst into tears....

A family was renting a three-bedroom home and appeared before me in an eviction hearing for non-payment of their rent.

When I questioned the parents about their refusal to make rental payments, they offered me a rather fetching picture of a squirrel sitting on a bed.

"Umm, cute," I observed. "Is he your pet?"

"This," said the father, "is why we won't pay our rent."

He went on to explain that all three bedrooms in the house are upstairs and that this wild rodent had taken up residence of the whole second floor. As a result, the family had abandoned the bedrooms to this cheeky invader and everyone was camping out on the main floor. Attempts to shoo the squirrel out an open window had only forced it to dig in and lay claim to his new home. Retrieving personal items from the second floor had become fodder for scary movies.

This might be fun for the kids for one night, but this situation had gone on for months and the landlord refused to send a squirrel wrangler to coax the little critter to live elsewhere.

I handed the picture to the landlord who stood sullenly nearby with his arms folded.

"What's wrong with this picture?" I challenged him.

A large retail store opened in our area and started having shoplifting issues. Greeters, trained in security, were quickly hired. Their ostensible job was to smile and welcome incoming customers and to scrutinize outgoing customers for unpaid items.

One Greeter was a bit mixed up on his duties. I discovered that when a customer walked into the store, he would greet the person warmly, then say with a smile: "Remember, if you're caught shoplifting in this store, Judge Conover is going to give you 90 days in jail!"

I suspect he was quickly told that this wasn't the welcome monologue that the store was expecting from him....

A Sargent from a local police department appeared in front of me to obtain an arrest warrant for a drunk driver.

The ticket had been written by another officer.

"I can't help but notice," I said to the Sargent, "that in fifteen years of being a judge here, I cannot remember this officer writing more than a couple of drunk driving tickets, despite the high incidence rate of drunk driving in the area he patrols."

The Sargent smiled and said: "You are right, Sir. He has only charged two offenders with drunk driving in the last fifteen years. In both cases," he added with a knowing grin: "the drunk smashed into the police car he was driving."

I was speaking to a group of young Drug Abuse Resistance Education (DARE) graduates at an elementary school when one boy raised his hand.

"Are you a *real* judge….you know, like Judge Judy?"

A man appeared before me on a charge of marijuana possession.

The man's job? Weed whacker at a cemetery.

That's why you don't take your work home with you….

One day I was packing my car to go turkey hunting when I heard a loud crash from the busy roadway near my home.

As I was checking on the injured motorist, another driver recognized me without my judicial robe and stopped his car and asked if he could help.

I appreciated the volunteering spirit of this driver, but I immediately recognized him as well...as the same guy I had just put on probation for driving with a suspended license.

I allowed the man to help direct traffic while everyone got medical attention and the damaged cars were towed away. Then, while the police swept up some glass, I ordered the Helper to walk home, and quit driving until he got his license issues straightened out.

"Ah, gee," grumbled the Good Samaritan with a teasing smile. "I thought sure you'd give me a break for helping out."

"I am." I replied. "I could have let you drive away...and then sent one of these fine officers after you."

I recently had a defendant in court for sentencing. He was about six feet, six inches tall. He was ashen faced when he stood for sentencing. He seemed to get the idea that he was headed for the slammer because suddenly he passed out and fell like a tree—splat to the floor.

Fortunately, the defendant cleared all the furniture obstacles in his descent and managed to fall without causing serious injury. When the paramedics revived him and he awaited his fate from the safety of a chair, I asked the age-old philosophical question: "If a tree falls in the forest and no one is around to hear it, does it make a sound?"

Unfortunately, the defendant was confused by philosophical thinking so I gave him plenty of time in jail to contemplate the answers to life's primal questions. And while he's at it, he could answer the more immediate question for himself: "If an idiot steals things when no one is around, is he still going to take a fall?"

A young man learned the hard reality of the Bible verse: Cast your bread upon the waters…and you will find it again.

Upset with his girlfriend, he threw a rock through her living room window. Startled and angry, she picked up the rock and threw it back through the hole in the window, unknowingly hitting her disgruntled boyfriend in the head.

When he was facing me later with a large bandage on his head, I pointed out to him that "Man reaps what he sows."

"Young man," I added: "you might try sowing wild oats instead of rocks…although it may not save you from even bigger headaches."

R eally, defendants are not that different from the rest of us. We all tend to gloss over our failures. Some defendants, however, take it to a new art form.

A man facing several serious charges, proudly announced to me in court that despite his many shortcomings (including the charges he was currently facing), he had at least stayed clean from cocaine since his arrest for it twenty years ago.

I congratulated him on this declaration and then examined the police report from the recent arrest.

"Wow," I told him. "This is interesting. You must have been wearing the same pair of pants at the time of this arrest that you had on twenty years ago…because this police report says you had cocaine in your pants pockets when you were picked up…. Those pants must have an incredible shelf life!"

A nother man with similar self-delusion was being sentenced by me on a charge of driving on a suspended license. He also declared his abstinence…this time from alcohol:

"Your honor," he said forcefully. "I haven't had a drink in fifteen years and I've been in the process of trying to get a new license ever since that drunk driving case fifteen years ago!"

After my sentencing, he was leaving the court when someone reported to our staff that the "teetotaler" reeked of alcohol.

I had him brought back into court where he flunked a breathalyzer test.

"Amazing!" I told the man. "That last drink you had fifteen years ago was a doozy! You're still drunk from it!"

S till another young man was arraigned in my court on drug charges. During his arraignment, he kept a baseball hat on his head which I advised him to remove. He was very reluctant to take it off, claiming that it was his lucky hat and he wore it everywhere.

I informed him that this court isn't "everywhere;" that there's no baseball game in sight and the sun isn't in anybody's eyes. Furthermore, that removing his hat demonstrates proper respect for the legal system and the law. Begrudgingly, he removed it.

As he was being taken across the hall to commence his journey to the county jail, the Police Chief got suspicious about the way the young man clung to the hat.

Upon examination, the Chief found illegal drugs stuffed into his interior hatband.

"I would say," declared the Chief to the young man: "You… and your lucky hat… have run plumb out of luck."

To prove that criminals aren't very inventive, I sentenced a defendant to jail on a drunk driving charge. When he was taken back to the lock-up, he was clutching a hat in his hand. Normally, he would just surrender his street clothes into a secure container that he could pick up at the end of his incarceration. However, his insistence on clinging to what he called his "Lucky Fishing Hat," made the deputies suspicious.

On closer inspection of the hat, several marijuana joints were discovered under the hat band. He was brought right back to court and arraigned on the new charges.

"Sir," I addressed him, "you may want to rename that hat."

A confused defendant thought he was being charged with Reckless Driving because he "recked" his car.

I was in a local sporting goods store buying shotgun shells for an upcoming hunting trip. At the checkout counter I turned around and found two very big guys—black beards, black cowboy hats, and glowering black eyes fixated directly on me. One was carrying a musket shotgun that he was evidently intending to purchase.

I couldn't escape the negative vibes coming my way so I greeted them warmly with a "Hello fellas."

Musket Carrier growled back at me: "We know who you are. Years ago you put my brother Harold here in the slammer. We ain't forgot you."

"Interesting," I replied with a cheerful smile as if we had renewed an old friendship.

Still smiling my nervous smile, I leaned over to the clerk and whispered to him: "That's my white car in the parking lot. Do me a favor and watch me walk out of here. If these guys follow me out to kiss me goodbye, call 911."

A retired educator that I work out with at a local fitness center was very distressed one night when I met up with him in the gym.

He had been to a wedding and some people there had mistakenly thought he was me, a situation that had he often faced.

"John, I'm just a quiet guy, not looking for trouble. You've got a target on the back of your robe. Man, I don't need that!"

"It's simple." I said. "Carry around a little stack of 'Get Out of Jail

Get out of jail free

Free' cards and give one of them to anyone who mistakes you for me.

"With my reputation, they'll know immediately that you're an imposter."

A defendant was standing in front of me and behind the podium. I asked him to raise his right hand to swear to tell the truth. He cleared his throat and looked uncertain.

I asked him, again, to raise his right hand. I even raised my right hand as an example as to what I wanted him to do. An awkward few seconds passed and then he stepped from behind the podium. I was quite embarrassed to see that he did not have a right arm.

I quickly raised my left hand and he followed.

"Does it still work with the wrong hand, Judge?" he asked.

"Oh, yes! If you break a left-handed oath to tell the truth," I replied, "we double the sentence."

I think he may have believed me….

A lady had her car's brakes replaced at a brake establishment business. She appeared in my court when she sued the establishment for faulty work.

Her testimony was that the day after the installation of the new brakes, they began squealing like the old brakes had done. She immediately returned to the brake shop where they claimed to "adjust" the new brakes. Within hours, the squeal was back.

The lady reported that she returned to the brake store five times for "adjustments," without ridding her car of the squealing.

Finally, the lady went to a competitor brake repair shop and had new brakes installed. The squeal never returned.

The defending brake shop owner testified that the squeal the lady kept hearing when she drove the car was "in her imagination." That was the totality of his defense.

My reply to the man was: "Sir, my choice is (a) to believe that this lady imagined running into a squealing pig every time she drove with your brakes on her car (a mental condition which was magically cured by new brakes from another shop) OR (b) to believe your brakes were defective and you refused to replace them."

"Sorry, Sir," I concluded: "I oink going with choice (a)."

A landlord was suing a tenant for eviction based on the tenant possessing a dog in violation of the lease agreement. She lived in an upstairs apartment and vehemently swore to me that she didn't own a dog or any other pet. "Have you ever seen this dog?" I asked the landlord.

He freely admitted that he had tried to catch the dog on the property, but had failed to do so. Whenever he showed up at her door, the dog wasn't to be seen and her lease prohibited him from searching her apartment without her permission, except in an emergency. She had refused that permission.

"I give up." I confronted the landlord. "What basis do you have for believing that the dog exists?"

"Well, Your Honor," he answered "in addition to neighbors claiming to hear occasional barking coming from her apartment, I have some other information."

At this point, the tenant's downstairs neighbor offered his testimony that for several days his ceiling had leaked right on his head while he was watching television. He thought it was toilet water from above. It smelled bad and it happened several times a day. He complained to the landlord who sent out a maintenance worker to investigate the problem.

What the maintenance man discovered was that the leak was coming in an area far from any plumbing in the defendant's upper apartment. So the maintenance man tested the liquid leak and, much to the neighbor's disgust, determined it was pet urine.

From the look on the tenant's face, I knew she had been "outed" by her "invisible" dog.

To say that I'm slow in coming to the technology age is more than a little accurate. My computer skills are minimally functional. I have only the vaguest idea what all the facebooking and twittering are about. My wife, who is very competent in technology, claims I haven't yet figured out how to use the hold button on our landline phone (maybe true, I'm not saying).

I can use the court's computer, which is strictly tied into my county's court system, to see my cases and read the court-generated emails. I can even do a little research for court documents on the court's computer.

One day in my court chambers, I looked at my system email account and a huge black-lettered banner appeared across my monitor screen threatening me with being ousted from the court's computer system. The wording was quite forceful (I might even add a bit rude) that I had violated some important usage norm, but I had no idea what I had done wrong.

I did the only sensible thing. Since my 10-year-old grandson wasn't available, I went and got a young clerk who was more comfortable on a computer than a duck hunter in hip boots.

She was pretty astonished to find out that I hadn't deleted any emails in the four years I had been using the court system, and I had managed to fill some memory chip (whatever that is) to the point that I was threatening the entire program. That omission had resulted in the unfriendly black banner on my screen. I shrugged and told her that I had no idea how to delete an email and learning how to do so was of complete disinterest to me.

"Delete it. Erase it. Tweet it. Hit it with a fly swatter." I grouched. "Just get rid of that black banner so I can read all those unnecessary email messages."

"Judge," she laughed: "Don't you ever send emails or reply to them?"

"That's what the telephone is for." I grumbled. "When I have something to say, I call people. I don't have to delete phone calls."

Three years later, the same banner appeared on my monitor screen.

"Katrina!"

A rather nice family restaurant in our area is right next door to a motel that, sadly, has often been the site of drug activities.

I arrived at the restaurant early one morning to speak to a Kiwanis Club which meets there weekly. Because the restaurant is a popular breakfast spot, I had to park next door in the motel's lot. I pulled in just as my female court administrator parked next to me. We stood and talked for a few minutes and then walked over to the restaurant together. We were unaware that the State Police had set up a stake-out on the motel, complete with cameras to record the comings and goings of suspected drug dealers.

When the police reviewed their tapes, it appeared that my court administrator and I could have been making a drug deal in the motel parking lot and then walking over to the restaurant for a little breakfast. It took a few hours for the police to correctly identify us, and that began several weeks when I was targeted by them for delighted teasing.

"I don't know, Judge," they would chortle at me: "The camera doesn't lie. Did we see you pull something out of your pocket in that video?"

"Yeah: some of my grandkids' bubble gum."

That's what blew my cover....

One of our local parks has a five mile running/walking track. A man drove to the park and sauntered off for his daily exercise.

Coming back to his car he realized he had locked his keys in the vehicle and called police, rather than his road service, to unlock the car. Though the police don't regularly do this service, they came and unlocked the vehicle for him.

When the door opened, the police were struck by an over-powering smell of marijuana.

Ooops. It seems the runner, in his frustration to get into his vehicle, forgot about several bags of the leafy substance in the trunk, and about who he had summoned for help.

Of course, the fact that he had liberally sampled his stash before the run (more likely a "meander") probably led him to forgetfulness.

Two officers made an arrest following a robbery at a convenience store.

The suspect, who became very unruly, was wrestled into a squad car by the two officers where the suspect continued to be combative.

One of the officers pulled out his mace to spray the suspect. The man ducked at the moment of truth and the second officer, struggling with the suspect from the other door, got a face full of mace.

Guess who escaped.

Who knew that police target practice should include *not* macing your partner....

H ard economic times have affected court systems too. Oftentimes our staff is short-handed from layoffs. To help, my Court Reporter and I often pitch in to open, sort, and distribute incoming mail, especially early in the week when the incoming mail is very heavy.

One busy Monday, my court reporter brought several stacks of mail into my office and we began tearing into it.

After a few minutes, something didn't seem right and I discovered that we had been opening the *outgoing* mail that was waiting to be picked up by the mail carrier.

Now when we offer our help to the staff, they are eager to declare that they have everything under control. Mail sorting is definitely above my pay grade....

My local courtroom is in a complex that also houses the City Hall and the local Police Department.

Our city mayor had arranged to perform a wedding in the City Hall: something she seldom did since she was also an ordained minister and preferred to do weddings in churches. However, in a phone conversation with the city clerk, the bride and groom pushed for a nondenominational setting. So the mayor not only agreed to perform the ceremony at City Hall, she decided to surprise them with a small cake, candles and music since several guests were also expected to attend this "informal" wedding.

I was in my chambers, minding my own business, when one of my clerks came back to tell me that a large wedding party had arrived for their wedding.

The wedding wasn't on our docket, but I assumed it was an oversight, so I told the clerk to bring everyone into the courtroom and that I would be happy to perform the wedding.

Unbeknownst to me, the mayor, probably no more than fifty feet away, was pacing the floor and fuming that this same wedding party had not appeared.

I finished the wedding, stuck around for pictures, and eventually ushered everyone on their celebratory way. Unfortunately, the mayor, a large woman with a booming voice, saw the wedding party leaving my courtroom. All of a sudden, a very angry mayor burst through the door—mad that I had "hijacked" her wedding! Despite my protestations of innocent mix-up, she followed with a string of personal denunciations which I considered to be rather "nondenominational" in nature. When I smiled and asked for a piece of her cake, she stormed off to box it up and blow out her mood candles.

I was forever-after eyed suspiciously by the mayor and she took great pains to guard all future ceremonies from the "Wedding Snatcher."

I'm innocent, I tell ya!

I received a late-night call for a search warrant for an alcohol blood test. These are usually done when someone is too injured in an accident to submit to a breathalyzer test, or who refuses a breathalyzer test and the officer has reason to believe the person is legally impaired (for instance while driving). Drawing blood in these situations demands a search warrant which is usually signed by a judge.

The original report called into 911 was that a person on a motorcycle was seen traveling at a high rate of speed on the highway, must have lost control, probably flipped over several times and crashed into the ditch. Witnesses came upon the scene and a body appeared to be nearby.

When the officer arrived at the scene, a person was indeed sprawled out on the side of the road, motorcycle on its side. The first thing out-of-order at the scene was the fact that the person was lying on a blanket. And although the motorcycle was still running and the headlight glaring, it seemed to be unharmed. The odor coming from the loudly snoring body told the rest of the story.

The drunken motorcyclist apparently understood his condition, pulled off the road, laid his cycle gently on its side, pulled out a blanket, and curled up indifferently to the speeding traffic just a few feet away, and went fast asleep.

As further proof that criminals are seldom geniuses, a young man committed a nighttime armed robbery of a party store while dressed from head-to-toe in black.

The officer, warned by a hidden panic button, was quickly on the scene as the robber fled the store on foot and headed for a nearby woods. The officer took off and chased him into the dark night, plunging through the thick vegetation.

"Wow," I exclaimed to the officer. "How in the world did you find him?"

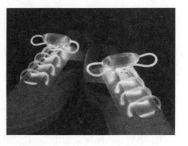

"It really wasn't as hard as I thought it was going to be," the officer smiled. "He was wearing running shoes that lit up with every step...."

It's sometimes ridiculously easy to "run afoul" of the law. A visitor to one of our local county parks was charged with destruction of park property. I was expecting some serious vandalism to be involved as I began to question the young man in court.

He explained that as he entered the park in his big truck (his pride and joy), the dirt road was wet from a recent rain. He gunned it through a depression in the road that had become a big puddle, spinning his wheels several times before making it across. Where the fun in this story went south was when the man realized that he had sprayed mud all over a Park Ranger's unmarked car.

The Ranger, either bored, grumpy, or his team had just lost the playoffs, stormed over to the defendant's truck and gave him a ticket for "destruction of the mud puddle." The young man pointed out that the mud puddle had settled back down into its normal deep and gushy state, but the Ranger was in no mood for logic.

As I dismissed the case, the young man said: "Judge, that hole has been in the same spot for years and I can't avoid hitting it when I visit that park. Could I ticket the Park Ranger for not filling it in?"

Don't push your luck, Son.

woman was brought into court, totally stressed out, to be arraigned on a retail fraud charge. When I asked her how she pled, she nearly screamed (and I directly quote):

"I am mentally and physically disabled, Your Honor! Because I have children!"

After hearing thousands of cases and listening to excuses of every kind to explain why people do the crazy/illegal/stupid/unwise things they do, I finally had a woman plead guilty without excuse. When pressed, she offered her philosophy of life:

"Stay humble and take each day as it comes."

I offered her my philosophy of life:

"Stay humble and take each day by the throat."

A pest exterminator was in court on a case, and proudly described himself as an External Infestation Control Expert. He does not, he stated emphatically, kill indoor bugs!

Fascinated, I asked him if indoor and outdoor bugs were different. What about country bugs and city bugs? Could an exterminator also be a bugcologist? Do indoor and outdoor exterminators have different certifications? Do you wear a different uniform? Do you study for this profession or do a bugalong with an expert? Do you have to trap the good bugs and relocate them to a safer habitat?

Even the External Infestation Control Expert ended up confused when our conversation ended, but the spectators seemed to have enjoyed the exchange....

You never know where a hero will appear from in the whacky world of court hearings.

A Contempt of Court hearing on a domestic assault and battery case was in progress. As these cases typically go, emotions throughout this hearing were at the explosion point.

At the conclusion of the hearing, the Defendant, his attorney, the ex-wife, her boyfriend, the mutual kids, and several witnesses all jumped up and started pointing fingers and yelling at each other.

My relatively new court reporter, a feisty young woman with plenty of street smarts, immediately recognized impending trouble and pushed an emergency button that called for help from the deputies on duty.

But, much to my surprise and before I could make a move myself, my court reporter jumped up and plowed into the middle of the fray, and began forcefully ordering people to sit down and shut up! Seconds later when eight Deputies burst through the doors with guns drawn, they found everyone sitting, seething, but with lips pinched shut, and a determined young court reporter standing firmly in their midst, daring anyone to start another outburst.

"Wow," I heard one deputy comment: "There must be a new sheriff in town."

A local bar owner is well known and active in our community. He sponsors many local sports teams, is generous with his assets, and often anonymously helps others who are down on their luck.

I consider this man a friend and I heard that he had been quite ill. So one morning, about 10:30, I stopped by the bar to see how he was feeling.

When I walked into the bar, I was surprised to see a number of men who were on probation to me for drunk driving. My surprise was only surpassed by theirs! I heard a few outcries and guttural cussing from the sparse crowd who *had been* enjoying a liquid breakfast.

> # NO
> # SOLICITORS
> ## or
> # JUDGES
> ## ALLOWED
> ## In the Bar

The bar owner came out and took me into his office where we discussed his improving recovery. I was happy to see him doing so well, and settled in for a few minutes to talk sports and politics.

"Judge," he finally said: "I sure appreciate your coming by, but how long you gonna stay? You know, you're really bad for business!"

He added with a uproarious laugh: "I'd hate to tell people that I had to kick the Judge outta my bar!"

I was raised in Southern Illinois where I spent many happy days hunting with my father and other relatives. Among the game we pursued included dove hunting, a very popular sport in that area of the country even though doves are an extremely difficult game to bag.

More recently, as I was approaching a re-election, I went on a pheasant hunt with a state senator friend who was also up for re-election. As we tromped through the fields, we discussed the fun (and difficulty) of dove hunting which was still not legal in Michigan.

For many years, the Michigan legislature had periodically considered legalizing dove hunting, so my senator friend decided it was time to lobby for its legalization. He came up with the brainstorm to contact an outdoor writer for our local newspaper that he knew pretty well and sell him on a feature article.

The article would include a "famous senator" who favors dove hunting and a local judge who would spin his idyllic childhood memories around the virtuous sport of hunting doves.

The meeting with the outdoor writer was quickly set up for the following week. However, days before our meeting, a statewide newspaper published a poll showing 93% of state residents opposed dove hunting....

Did I mention I was approaching a re-election?

End of article. End of lobbying for dove hunting.

A father appeared before me with a sad and amazing story. He had (unwisely, I would say) loaned a substantial sum of money to his adult daughter who had already proven herself to be unreliable and irresponsible. But as a father, I can understand parental compassion, even when it defies logic.

Time went on and the daughter made no effort to repay her father or to show any signs of straightening out her life.

At an extended family get-together, father and daughter both drank and argued about the money throughout the day. (So obviously Dad is not guilt-free in this story).

At the end of the family event, the daughter finally agrees to pay her father back and directs him to follow her to the bank where she can withdraw money for him. So (even more unwisely) off they go in each of their cars.

Mile after mile, passing bank after bank, the daughter leads her father in a parade around the county. When Dad starts honking and yelling out the window, he is soon stopped by the police and arrested for drunk driving *and stalking*!

When the confusion was all sorted out, Dad found out his daughter had called 911 and reported that some drunk had been following her, and harassing her for several hours.

So Dad was out the money. Out of luck driving drunk. And disqualified for the "Father of the Year" award. Sort of a trifecta of stupid....

Most of us already know that legislators, both state and federal, have too much time on their hands and think that it's their primary job to pass new laws and regulations by the tankerload. Hence we have little kids who can't sell lemonade in their front yards and teachers who think they can't have classes recite the Pledge of Allegiance.

A young man didn't want to sell lemonade, but he did like to catch snapping turtles and raise them, apparently with loving care. So far, so good (amazingly!). However, he became a hardened criminal when he tried to sell a snapper on a commercial website. The DNR (Department of Natural Resources in Michigan) swooped in on our felon, informing him that selling snapping turtles requires a license!

"Let me get this straight," I addressed the DNR officer and the turtle trafficker in court. "These are the same turtles that people in cars go out of their way to squash, and fishermen put in soup. This is the turtle that kids run from? And they have to be protected from the cruelties of turtle swapping???"

People think that domestic violence usually involves stories of cheating or arguing over money. I have found that many of them are sparked by ludicrous reasons.

A young man and woman who lived together were in the process of cooking dinner when a fight broke out resulting in assault and battery charges against the boyfriend. When I questioned the man to explain what set off these events, he complained that his girlfriend was cooking stirfry and he was annoyed by the loud sizzle.

Say what?

Another romantic young couple started a domestic spat with angry words, followed by pushing and shoving, then fisticuffs. It quickly escalated to throwing bricks (I held back from asking about how the bricks came to be handy). And when the police arrived, each was trying to find the household gun and the bullets which (thankfully) were stored separately.

When questioned, neither lovebird could clearly recall what started this, but a few hours previous to this, they were willing to kill one another over it!

R ight before Christmas I was calling out cases in court by first and last names.

I called: "Nicholas Smith!"

No answer.

Again: "Nicholas Smith!"

No answer.

"Well," I said: "is Jolly Old St. Nicholas here?"

Several people raised their hands.

[An aside from Karen: John loves Christmas and giving presents, but... well you see what you think:]

J ohn to me: "You'll never guess in a hundred years what I'm giving you for Christmas."

To be honest, these arc words to chill a woman's heart. (Hint: ask yourself if there could be a good reason *why* I would never guess this present!).

Just before Christmas, my husband came forth with this happy pronouncement, the same one that he says nearly every year: "If you made out a hundred wish lists, Buttercup, what I'm giving you wouldn't be on it."

I refrain again this year, in the face of his self-satisfied smile, from responding with, "If it's not on any of my lists, what makes you think I want it?"

Cobras aren't on any of my lists. PVC piping isn't on my lists. Reindeer antler hats aren't on my lists. Fake dog-doo isn't on my lists. Fish pillows aren't on my lists. A plastic moose that ejects chocolate pellets from his tail isn't on my lists. In fact, I

don't pine for ANYTHING that isn't on at least *one* my lists....
My husband, however, puts a great premium on surprises in
gift-giving. It trumps need or even desire. Maybe it's from suf-
fering the scars of childhood Christmases when he was inflicted
with cruel presents like socks, underwear and Gene Autry pajamas. I don't know.

Whatever the reason, it has caused him to mistake "astonish-
ment" for "delight" when people open what he calls his "original" gifts. Nothing makes him happier than seeing a gift recipi-
ent's frozen smile of puzzlement. A gift that you can actually
use, he considers "boring."

His determination to achieve surprise has reached such limits that I refuse to make out a wish list for him. I used to give
him lists because he asked for one. I'm a slow learner. After
years of this, I finally realized that he used those wish lists to
eliminate gift choices. If he gave me what I put on my lists, I
wouldn't be SURPRISED!

Okay. I freely acknowledge that the Non-
surprise Christmas gift has gotten out
of control in our culture. A
friend of mine says that
his family exchanges
identical checks in the
mail. Still other fami-
lies exchange equivalent
gift cards: here's your $50 gift card; thank you for my $50 gift
card. (You shouldn't have!). I must admit, surprises are better
than that.

Mary and Joseph must have been pretty surprised when the
Wise Men showed up at the stable. Shepherds hanging around
might be unusual, but decked-out Kings from the Orient had to
be mind-boggling to a small-town carpenter and his teenage wife.

And the presents! Wow! What Mary probably really could have used was a few diapers and a fleece blanket. A gift basket of fruit and cheese would have come in handy after that long journey. What she got was gold, and exotic oils of frankincense and myrrh.

Do you think that even once Mary thought: "What in the world am I going to do with this stuff? How will we fit those things on the donkey?"

The greatest surprise gift of all, of course, was Christ Jesus himself. And it's the sacrifice of His incredible love that we feebly imitate at Christmas when we exchange gifts. Chia pets and all.

I'm happy (yes, and even thankful) that husbands, and God Himself, like to surprise us with their expressions of love.

Yah. That's on my list.

farmer's cows kept escaping to a neighbor's field causing weekly complaints.

It finally ended up in court where there was a hearing in front of me. During my ruling, I couldn't resist quoting the old proverb: "The grass is always greener on the other side of the fence," to explain the cows' behavior.

"In that case," grumbled the neighbor. "When those darn cows are in *my* field, why can't I get them to look over the fence and go home?"

L ate one evening in our public park, a man was rowing his boat across the lake. Proving that it isn't only driving a car that shouldn't be done under the influence of alcohol, he stood up in his small boat, capsizing it and throwing him some distance from the overturned boat.

The man couldn't swim so he began screaming for help.

Two fishermen on the shore swam out and pulled our seafarer to shallow water. They pulled him up the bank and pumped the water out of his lungs.

A Park Ranger who had witnessed the whole event from a distance, soon arrived on the scene and decided that the man's yelling for help violated the park's noise ordinance, thus disturbing the peace.

"Evidently," I told the rescued boater, "you should have gone ahead and drowned quietly.

"Of course, then you might have been charged with polluting the lake."

There's an unwritten rule among all drunk drivers. I could be wrong. The rule may be a framed needlepoint over every bar in town and a label on every case of beer:

All I know is that every time I ask a person charged with drunk driving how many drinks he or she had, the answer is always:

"Two!" or "I only had a couple a drinks." This, regardless of how high their breathalyzer or blood test registered for alcohol.

So I wasn't surprised when I asked a woman about how many beers she had drunk before getting in her car. She came up with the standard answer. I then pointed out her high blood alcohol content and asked her how big these two beers were.

In a rare display of semi-honesty, she smiled sheepishly and said: "They were probably each about two feet tall and two feet wide."

"I give up," I countered. "Were you bobbing for fermented apples?"

"Yes, Your Honor," she laughed. "But I only ate a couple of 'em!"

To prove that drinking doesn't solve anyone's problems, we can take a look at the woman who spent hours in a local bar drowning what she considered to be her sorrows.

After enough booze to pickle a rhinoceros, she stumbled outside and plopped down on the steps of the bar. Somehow, through her haze she realized that she shouldn't drive. Maybe she just couldn't focus well enough to find her car.

At any rate, she was able to fish out her cellphone and call 911 for help. When the police arrived, instead of getting a YourRide home from the police, she was arrested for public intoxication.

Sorrows aren't gone.

Paycheck blown on booze.

Night in the county jail with not-nice people.

Bad headache and smelly clothes in the morning.

Facing a grumpy judge.

Large attorney and fine fees.

Thin silver lining: she didn't drive drunk and kill someone.

But, sorrows still aren't gone.

When people fail to appear in court, a warrant is issued for their arrest. Many soon realize that they had better report to a probation officer before they are nabbed in a routine traffic stop and get hauled off to jail.

However, even after reporting to a probation officer, they often get cold feet and run out before facing their court hearing. My probation officers were getting quite disgusted with these birds of flight who go back on the run.

Finally, a creative probation officer had a man turn himself in on a warrant. She explained to the man that he would have to come into Court with her and face the music. He suddenly announced that he had to go to the bathroom, located near the exit—the common ploy to escape.

Ready for this ruse, the probation officer said: "Okay, fine. Give me your billfold. When you come back, you, your billfold, and I will go see Judge Conover."

A man appeared in court charged with allowing his dog to run loose. The dog? A rather large bull dog.

I asked him the dog's name and he replied: "Sergei Fedorov." [a famous former hockey player]

"Really," I said. "What made you pick that name?"

"Well, first Your Honor, his face reminds me of a hockey player. And, second, he leaves a lot of 'pucks' around the yard."

"Interesting," I laughed.

"But Sergei needs to keep himself and his pucks in his home rink.

"Otherwise," I added, "you and Sergei will be sent to the penalty box."

I was in a local restaurant eating lunch one day during the O.J. Simpson trial.

I asked the waitress for the bill, and she pointed out a couple walking to their car and said that they had paid for my lunch.

I explained that I don't accept lunches, but since the couple was driving away, I really didn't have a choice.

The waitress explained that the couple said they had been in my court for several hours following their own court business. They simply stayed to watch "the show."

"They said," continued my waitress, "that you could have finished the O.J. Simpson trial in a few days and saved the taxpayers millions of dollars."

Thanks. But TV would have missed millions of entertainment dollars without that dragged-out soup opera. Just like ancient Rome offered its subjects bread and circuses, I guess you could say that someone bought my bread and America got the circus....

During my years on the bench, and during my twenty years of being a general practice attorney before that, I noticed that people in unhappy relationships always seemed to need an "excuse" to finally walk away. Unhappiness was never enough to move them out of their "comfort" zones, even when the zones were anything but comfortable.

Of course, the most popular, noncreative excuse people use to break up an existing relationship is finding someone else. The someone else is usually not the answer they are seeking, but it is excellent for wrecking any current relationship.

A young man's live-in girlfriend evidently rejected this age-old, tried and true method of dumping your lover. She squawked on her boyfriend by reporting his illegal possession of a crow to the DNR (Department of Natural Resources), a transgression with penalty fines up to $1,000.

The ratted-out boyfriend appeared before me.

When I asked him to explain his situation, he was blunt: "I let the crow fly away, and kicked out my birdbrain girlfriend."

Let freedom ring....

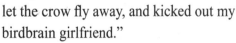

I've preformed many weddings over the years, many in the summer. One such summer wedding was planned to take place in someone's attractive backyard.

The wedding day dawned bright and sunny; a blessing indeed in Michigan. I took my place along with the groom and listened to a small group of musicians playing *I Love You Truly.*

A few minutes before the ceremony was to begin, a cool wind picked up and dark clouds seemed to appear out of nowhere. Just as the crowd rose to *Here Comes the Bride*, the rain drops began to fall.

The bride steeled herself and began to navigate the red-runnered path toward her groom. The wind whipped higher and the rain began in earnest. The musicians ran for cover but the guests seemed determined to respect the bride's decision to forge ahead so they froze in place, but everyone was soon drenched.

I plowed through the wedding vows at top speed, but not before the torrents transformed the bride into sloppy dishevelment. A beautiful hairdo came loose and drizzled down her head. Her carefully applied makeup job turned into dark puddles that slid down her face. The bottom of her lovely dress was covered with mud, and all the fluffy lace and tulle went flat as a pancake.

The groom didn't fare any better, but still had a big smile on his face. When I declared them "Man and Wife" with the speed of an auctioneer, and the guests began turning over chairs in their haste to get inside, the two drowned lovebirds ignored the plight of the situation and kissed each other long and passionately.

I bet they're still laughing about their soggy wedding…and still loving each other.

For better or worse.

[Aside from Karen: You may have noticed on the back cover that John and I have been married for fifty years. (I'm not denying the rumor that I was three-years-old when we married!). We are often asked for our marital wisdom, so here it is:]

Sauerkraut and Polish sausage.

That's our best advice if you're planning a wedding reception any time soon.

I readily admit our research is unscientific, but John and I have been mulling over the sad divorce numbers for young couples today—and in the public interest, and because together we have one hundred years of experience!, we decided to find the key to successful marriage…and pass it on. Besides, it really saddens John when he spends hours of his life performing wedding ceremonies at Hooty-Tooty wedding venues, only to find out a few years later that the love birds are divorced!

We quickly ruled out big, elaborate weddings as the guarantor of eternal bliss. In fact, we reflected on the fact that the cost of many weddings today equals the GNP for Puerto Rico, and still the giddy couple's passion cools off before the beef flambé does.

John and I concluded (again, quite unscientifically) that the more expensive the champagne, and the plumper the fresh strawberries around the decadent chocolate fountain, the more likely the newlyweds will end up fattening the portfolio of a divorce lawyer…probably before the over-priced caterer is paid off. And more than one meat entrée is definite marital suicide! And don't get us started about wedding cake so expensive that they have to cut it with a cheese slicer!

We can't conclusively give you the reason for this phenomenon. Maybe it has to do with the reality of married life after the free-fall from the outer galaxy of a fantasy wedding. It's a long way, baby, from champagne and out-of-season strawberries to toilet bowl cleaners. Maybe too far to come without injury.

Nope, I can assure you: everyone we ever knew who had sauerkraut and polish sausage at their wedding reception, along with home-made sheet cakes that can be served in great slabs, is still happily married.

John points out that "cake and punch in the church hall" weddings are also very durable (which worked for us!). And it has the added benefit that you learn who your real friends are since only they will attend a meal-less reception. Even our cousins tried to pretend they were too busy to attend our nuptials when they found out the punch wasn't spiked!

John does admit that he is partial to weddings with food and foolish dancing. But then he adds: "But, if you really want to guarantee marital longevity, serve venison at the wedding reception. It has dozens of advantages! The groom gets to hunt the entrée with his buddies (which nicely precursors what he'll be doing *after* the wedding). It doesn't cost anything beyond a hunting license, so you can afford a honeymoon Up North (a preview of future family vacations). And you'll have some meat left over for the freezer when you get home from touring Escanaba in black fly season."

I guess I reluctantly agree with John. However, I must add this warning. A venison reception nearly failed once. My friend's cousin from Muskegon tried to put an uptown cosmopolitan twist on it and served venison *chop suey* at her wedding reception. Her in-laws thought she was putting on airs. Her embarrassed parents suffered weeks of ribbing at the VFW hall, and her new husband couldn't face his hunting buddies for several months.

So…if you're not familiar with the niceties of serving venison, it's probably best to just stick to sauerkraut and Polish sausage….

Sto lat!

From the annals of "I can't make this stuff up," I was arraigning a man and advising him of his rights concerning the pending criminal charges against him.

He was charged with putting out a larger-than-allowed bait pile for attracting deer. Furthermore, he was found in possession of a deer carcass that he had not legally tagged.

I repeated my explanations to him several times to make sure he understood the charges, but he continued to smile calmly and I was concerned that he didn't grasp the gravity of his situation.

Finally, I asked him if he had any questions. He continued to smile, and in front of a packed courtroom, he pulled a package out of a bag near his feet and offered it to me.

"I know you're a hunter," said the man. "So I brought you some venison."

It took me several seconds to believe what I had just heard. And the audience all seemed to be holding their breaths.

Finally, I replied: "Mr. Smith, this sounds suspiciously like another attempt at illegal baiting."

Deer me!

I was eating lunch several times a week at one of my favorite local restaurants. A new waitress began serving me and, no matter what item I ordered, it always seemed a little bigger than usual. Little extra items appeared with every order. The sandwiches seemed a little thicker. My iced tea was refilled nearly after every swallow.

When I complimented the waitress to her boss, he gave me a hearty laugh:

"Judge, in a few days she is scheduled to appear in front of you on a drunk driving case. If it doesn't happen soon, she's going to clean out my kitchen feeding you!"

Military recruiters are always eager to help young men and women facing minor criminal charges to try to get the cases disposed of and get the young person on track for a successful future. In return for this help, the young person signs on the bottom line and goes off to boot camp. The recruiter gets a nice bonus for each new military recruit, and many young people have changed life courses for the better in this arrangement.

A young man still owed $500 in fines he couldn't pay, and expressed his eagerness to join the army.

The recruiter paid the $500 out of his own pocket and escorted the young man to a bus stop in Detroit to be shipped out. In the early morning hours, the young man was in line to board the bus with his helpful recruiter looking on.

Right before his turn to climb onto the bus, the young man turned abruptly and ran off into the night—not to be seen again.

The next day, the disgusted recruiter showed up at court and was trying to think of ways to track down his runaway recruit.

"My experience in rabbit hunt-  ing," I told him, "is that, once you see a rabbit, you can chase him till you and your dog drop in exhaustion. If you sit in one spot and wait, he'll circle around and come right back to you.

"My guess is that, sooner or later, we'll all see him again."

Many cases should never make it to court. People seem, not just quick to sue others, they often call 911 over silly stuff which they need to grow up and handle themselves.

A young man was brought into court charged with domestic assault on his girlfriend.

The two were sitting at the breakfast table when the young man picked up a muffin and "smooshed" (as opposed to "smashed") it in her face.

She called 911 as if she had been criminally violated, but she was now sitting in the court proceedings, showing some remorse for her hasty call.

When they appeared in front of me, he claimed to be just kidding around, and asserted that she had eaten half the muffin before she decided she had been assaulted.

"Are you planning on marrying this woman?" I asked.

He glanced in her direction: "Probably," he incredibly replied.

"Well, you might consider skipping the traditional cake-in-the-face smooshing ceremony if she's that offended by the muffin," I offered.

"I'm sure hoping," he said: "that she just doesn't like blueberries."

At the scene of an armed robbery, one of the officer's dogs chased down the suspect and got in a few good bites before the officers cuffed him.

When the defendant complained to me about his injuries, he found little sympathy.

"The dog was just doing his part to take a bite out of crime...."

Late one evening, a man was arrested on a drunk driving charge when he went through a McDonald's drive-through... the wrong way!

When the man appeared before me, I noted his very high blood alcohol level reported by the arresting officer, and wondered if the man even remembered his arrest.

"Oh yes," he replied. "I was trying to return a cheeseburger that didn't have any pickles."

I'd say, he's short a few pickles himself....

P eriodically, I do a Night Court session. Law enforcement agencies around the county assemble all their existing warrants and go out knocking on doors to find the fugitives from justice. They are then brought into the court to face charges they have been avoiding.

A man was picked up in one of these round-ups and arrested for failure to have a dog license. He and the unlicensed dog were home alone when the police came calling late at night. The dog, he kept insisting, belonged to his girlfriend who was not home at the time. But, until this was straightened out, the man had to spend the night in jail.

The final irony: when the man was released, he discovered that his girlfriend was actually keeping the dog for its real owner... her new boyfriend! And while he sat in jail for Fido, she was out cavorting with boyfriend number two!

Arf!

T he police were called out to the scene of a domestic dispute. By the time they arrived, the husband had left the premises.

The next morning, the husband arrived at the local police station—with several boxes of donuts and coffee—to tell his side of the story....

S ome years ago, before I was appointed to the bench and was still practicing law, I went pheasant hunting with an old friend. We had permission to hunt on farm land near my sister's home, and we took my father's trusty (and free-spirited) black lab named Bear.

Unfortunately, the dog was fond of hunting not just pheasants, but most anything that struck his fancy, and he ended up racing off to sniff around someone's backyard who owned a coop full of chickens. Of course, we had to trudge over to this house, loaded guns and all, in an attempt to persuade Bear to rejoin the actual hunt.

By the time we caught up with Bear, he had flushed out several chickens who were squawking and flying in every direction. The property owner, a man of no nonsense and even less humor, took no time at all in calling the police on his intruders. Being a small community, the police cars came from every direction to get in on the action.

My friend and I set off to collar the dog who was having a wonderful time chasing around and around the man's house with chickens and feathers flying everywhere. Once nabbed, an officer directed Bear to the back of his police car where he happily jumped in.

My hunting buddy and I were soon in the back of another police car, trying to explain what was going on to a rookie cop who acted like he'd just busted up a crime syndicate.

My sister's home was in view of all the commotion, so my father walked down to see what all the fuss was about and found his dog sitting in the back of a police cruiser, and his son doing some fast talking.

My dad went back to my sister's house and announced to everyone waiting for a report on the neighborhood brouhaha, that Bear had been arrested and the family would probably have to raise bail for him. Apparently, I was on my own! Thanks, Dad.

I actually had to appear in front of a judge, charged with violating the ordinance against hunting in someone's back yard. I presented my story to the judge and then told him, in my most emphatic voice, that I took great offence to the police report which stated: "Mr. Conover and Mr. St. Onge were hunting with a loaded gun and dog."

"We did have our loaded hunting guns with us, Your Honor," I admitted. "But I categorically deny that the dog was loaded!!"

The judge laughed so hard that he dismissed the case.

One evening I was in my chambers preparing to go give a speech to a local Kiwanis Club.

The cleaning lady came in and I could tell that she was feeling down. She dragged herself from job to job, so I called her over and had her sit down. Even though I was running late, I told her I wanted to practice my speech and could I try out a few of my funny stories on her.

She laughed heartily at every story. She seemed to revive her good spirits, and I know it certainly made me feel good to make her laugh.

I made a mental note to try out all my material on that sweet cleaning lady; she even laughed at the stuff my wife said wasn't funny.... In fact she laughed at the stuff the Kiwanians didn't get.

It's obvious, the cleaning lady is a person of discerning good taste!

A woman that I had ordered to attend AA (Alcoholics Anonymous) meetings as part of her sentence, called and said she didn't want to go to any more meetings.

I asked her why and she said: "Man, *those* people have a lot of problems!"

Uhhh, yes *they* do! Which is why *you're* there.

A man was drinking at a local bar where his wife is the bartender.

They were having marital problems and, without his knowing it, his wife was dating somebody else. So despite all his efforts to talk with her, she ignored him and kept on pouring him extra strong drinks.

At closing time, she left with her boyfriend out the back door and the husband stumbled drunk out the front. She then called 911 and said that her husband was driving away from the bar drunk.

She spent the night with her boyfriend and he spent the night in jail.

There's a country song in there somewhere....

A man spent a good deal of his life robbing banks and party stores, and taking up space in prisons. During his non-jail time, he worked as an Elvis Presley impersonator.

"Isn't this taking *Jail House Rock* to an extreme?" I asked him when he was facing new charges. "You just got out of jail. Do I need to *Return to Sender*?"

A young man who was paralyzed from the waist down for many years after a youthful accident was returning home from church. He climbed alone into his specially equipped van which he had been competently driving for several years.

As he began to move out of the parking lot, apparently his special equipment malfunctioned and the car lurched into a tree, and he was severely injured.

The only eye witness to the event was a man who was exiting the church at the time and swore that the young man's account fit exactly what he witnessed from a few feet away.

In the law suit which followed against the equipment company, the young man's attorney listed the name of the single witness. It didn't look like a strong case to the legion of attorneys hired by the big equipment company.

The equipment company categorically refused to settle the case, sure that they could persuade a jury that the only witness wasn't being truthful, and he might have been in cahoots with the young man.

The day before trial, both parties informed me that the equipment company offered a generous settlement and the suit was withdrawn.

Maybe that big turn-around came when the equipment company found out that the solitary witness that they expected to expose as a partisan hack, was, in fact, the local Catholic priest.

Just guessing....

A defendant appeared in front of me on a very busy day. While I was pulling up his case, I asked him what happened.

He said that he was fishing with his dog, Spot. He described in some detail the day he had spent on the lake.

"Really," I replied. "Did you catch anything?"

"Yes Sir." He said sadly: "I caught a drunk driving ticket on the way home."

A woman showed up in court with three young children hoping that the sad looking children would prevent me from giving her jail time.

Her driving record was abysmal: repeated drunk driving offences, and this charge included injuring some innocent occupants in another vehicle.

After I put her in jail, the deputy had to take custody of the three young children. That's when he discovered that the children didn't belong to the defendant! She had borrowed them from her friends!

Good friends. Bad parents.

There isn't much funny that happens in drug raids. They are always very dangerous and even more unpredictable. The combination of weapons, drugs, and desperate bad guys is always a formula for trouble.

I had signed a warrant for a drug raid on a trailer residence that the police had under surveillance for weeks.

The police arrived late at night when all suspects had been spotted entering the home, and no one had been seen leaving. The police announced their presence on a bull horn and told everyone in the home to come out with their hands up.

No response.

After several attempts to rouse a response, the police got out their battering ram and prepared to blast through the door.

Just as they were about to rush the door, an old woman opened the door and gave the police "the finger," then slammed the door and locked it.

All the more irritated and determined, the police bulked up the manpower to use that battering ram to open the door. They sprang forward at top speed.

Just as the battering ram reached the front door, the old woman swung open the door and the bunched-up police, battering ram and all, flew through the open door and slammed completely through the picture window across from it, taking out half the wall, ending up in a pile of cops, guns, drugs, glass, furniture, suspects, and one barking dog, in a heap in the back yard.

Well, that was subtle.

The job of being a defense attorney is often very very difficult. They frequently have to defend the indefensible, and do it convincingly.

A defense attorney approached the bench to explain to me that his drunk driving client had driven off the road and smashed a mailbox. Still, he argued that his client was a good and responsible man who normally would not have acted in such a way. This is his first (and last, by golly!) offense. He's never even had a parking ticket! Besides, there was really no harm done. He was sure the mailbox was easily repaired.

After I let him ramble on about his "boy scout" client, I informed him that the smashed mailbox belonged to my Court Reporter's parents, who had indeed been inconvenienced and suffered the cost and labor of replacing the mailbox. The rebuffed attorney slunk back to his seat in stunned silence.

A few weeks later, the same lawyer appeared in court representing another client. The charge was the same: a drunk driving occurrence, and another smashed mailbox.

I motioned the lawyer to the bench.

"Um, Counselor," I said. "Guess whose brand new mailbox your client hit this time?"

Uh huh. My Court Reporter's parents.

A fellow judge was once a defense attorney who argued cases in front of me. The following is one of those cases which he recently described as one his most bizarre and most memorable:

At one time in the past, drunk driving cases had to come to trial within seventy-seven days of the arrest date, or they were subject to dismissal. This deadline was nearly impossible given the several legal steps that had to be accomplished before an actual trial.

A drunk driving case had finally wound its way to the day of trial. When the case finally came before me, all parties were there and ready for testimony and the jury had been seated.

However, right out of the box, the defense attorney (now a judge) and his client made a motion to dismiss the case because seventy-seven days had already passed.

The flustered prosecutor scrambled through a bunch of papers and found out that, indeed, seventy-seven days had passed.

I granted the request to dismiss the case based on that rule. I then dismissed the jury to return to the jury room. All smiles, the defense attorney began to pack up his briefcase and patted the back of his relieved client. The dejected prosecutor began reassembling his papers.

I ordered everyone to sit down, telling them that the court wasn't done with them yet. I then called the arresting officer to the podium and had him swear out a new warrant for the arrest of the defendant. I signed the warrant and the officer re-arrested the defendant on the spot. I then re-arraigned the stunned defendant, set the bond, and told the bailiff to bring back the jury.

The shocked, but quick thinking defense attorney, hoping to throw a monkey wrench in the direction I was going, jumped to his feet:

"Your Honor! He stammered: "We can't proceed! I haven't been hired yet on *this* case!"

"That's true, Counselor," I replied.

Then, turning to the defendant, I said: "If you can't afford an attorney in this case, I have several court appointed attorneys waiting in the hall on other matters. You can choose one of them, or you can choose to retain your former lawyer who is still sitting next to you.

"In any case, this trial is going forward in fifteen minutes."

It did.

L ate at night, a man snuck out of his house—leaving his wife peacefully sleeping in their bed—to meet his girlfriend at a local bar.

The two proceeded to drink an impressive amount of alcohol and were later stopped within sight of the girlfriend's house by a police officer for drunk driving.

The officer gave the couple a break. He sent the girlfriend home by foot and followed the man to his home, admonishing him to stay home with his wife and behave himself.

After a short time at home, the wandering husband snuck out again, got in his car, and took off toward his girlfriend's home.

The same officer pulled him over again for drunk driving and this time Mr. Cheater was not going to get a break. Off he went to jail.

A few days later, the man appeared in front of me to be arraigned on the drunk driving charges and, due to his driving record, I set a high bond on him.

Soon, the man's wife showed up to post bond so her beloved

husband wouldn't have to go to jail. She stopped at the clerk's counter to pay the bond and the clerk told the wife that she just might want to read the police report before she posted bond.

A few minutes into the read, the wife screamed in anger, threw the report on the floor, and stomped out of the courthouse leaving the playboy husband to be taken back to jail.

In a police report:

"When I checked the back seat of the suspect's car, I seized one bottle of Sour Apple Pucker that was ½ full and one bottle of Mohawk Vodka that was ½ empty."

I've had attorneys give an incredible variety of reasons for asking for adjourning a court hearing. Some of them are legitimate and some are a bit fishy.

The prize for uniqueness (and chutzpah!) goes to the attorney who requested an adjournment because her dog had puppies and she wanted to stay home for a few days to bond with them.

An attractive female defendant appeared in front of me for sentencing on a criminal case. She came to court dressed to impress: lots of makeup, hair carefully styled, outfit as revealing and sexy as she thought she could get away with. Her tight skirt didn't cover much real estate but it couldn't detract from the colorful scarf tied carefully around one ankle. I wondered if that was a new fashion trend.

A deputy tipped me off when he saw my confused look. He told me that the defendant was wearing a tether on her ankle as ordered by an-other judge on a previous charge...the same charge, different incident, that I was sentencing her for today. She was hoping I wouldn't notice the tether and become aware that she was a repeat offender.

The tether, something I never use, had not prevented her from committing another crime. That's why I never use it.

"Where I'm sending you, Miss Smith," I told her: "You'll be glad to know that you won't need that leg jewelry any longer.

"I'll see to it that it gets returned to the previous judge."

During our daughter's summer break from law school, she was working as an intern for the county prosecutor. She had a drunk driving trial in another court in which a local police officer had to testify. That evening, the same police officer called me to sign a search warrant on another drunk driving case.

I asked him how his trial had gone that morning. He replied that he had had trouble concentrating on his testimony because he couldn't keep his eyes off the cute new prosecutor.

Before I could comment, he went on to make a couple of lewd observations about her physical attributes, and he was sorry he didn't catch her name.

"Uh, Officer," I interrupted. "Her name was Bree Conover."

"Oh no!!!" He gasped. "Please tell me she's not your daughter!"

"I'm afraid I can't tell you that, Officer."

I never run into him that he doesn't choke and turn red.... Poor guy.

An officer broke up two men fighting outside a bar. It culminated in the officer whacking one defendant in the head with his nightstick.

At the defendant's trial, the defense attorney questioned the policeman who had swung the nightstick:

Q: Officer, did you deal my client a life-threatening blow to the head with a nightstick?

A: Yes Sir, I did.

Q: (Forcefully) Was that necessary?

A: Yes Sir, it was.

Q: (Snarling) And why is that?

A: He had my thumb in his mouth trying to bite it off.

Q: Officer! Don't you think you over-reacted?

A: Counsclor, lcan over here, put your thumb in my mouth, let me try to bite it off and let's see how long it takes you to hit me in the head.

Defense Attorney: No more questions.

A man was charged with illegally growing marijuana. An officer requested a warrant based upon a plant he found in the suspect's possession. I asked the officer what kind of plant he had found and he said wryly: "Potted."

Technology is changing every aspect of our lives, including arrests.

A young man was taken into custody for an outstanding arrest warrant. When he was handcuffed and put in the back seat of a police car, the officers overlooked confiscating his cell phone.

The young man was not only able to fish the phone out of his pocket, handcuffs and all, he somehow managed to send a text to his mother: "Hey Mom, I've been arrested on that old warrant!"

The officers became aware of the texting going on in the back seat when the man's text alert chime went off. Mom's reply: "You better save your texting for a bondsman. I told you to take care of that warrant!"

A nervous man appeared before me on a simple case of allowing his dog Peaches to run loose. He was also on a strict probation to me for a drunk driving charge.

"Your Honor," he said, wiping sweat from his brow: "does this dog running loose charge violate my probation in any way? I've tried so hard to do everything you gave me."

"Well, Joe. Were you or Peaches driving while she was on the run?" I asked.

"Oh, no Sir!"

"Were you or Peaches drinking alcohol before, during, or while the romp was going on?" I asked with mock earnestness.

"Never!" Joe replied emphatically.

"Then you're good to go, Joe. But I'm adding Peaches to your probation requirements. No drinking, driving, or running loose for either one of you."

"Thanks, Your Honor. My wife will be glad to hear that last part."

L ate on a Friday afternoon, a DNR (Department of Natural Resources) officer called the court. He had made an arrest and requested that I wait to arraign the person he had nabbed.

At 6 P.M., the court doors flew open and in came a tall woman, well over six feet tall. She was handcuffed and two crying children trailed behind her. The scowling DNR officer directed her my way, his hand menacingly on his handgun, and marched her up to the podium.

"What is the charge here, officer?" I asked.

"Fishing without a license!" he announced. She hung her head in shame.

I had her uncuffed, and calmed the children with some treats from the clerk's desk. As the story unfolded, she was a Nanny in charge of the two children in tow. The officer had to bring them along since they were with her at the lake.

After chatting with her about her catch, she asked me for an attorney. I granted that request, of course, and she was scheduled to reappear in a few days.

When she appeared back in front of me with her attorney, they produced evidence that she is a Native American, and therefore does not require a license to fish.

Case dismissed.

Before she left the court, she asked to give me a sheet of paper. On it she had drawn a map of the lake, marked with her favorite fishing holes, and listed her favorite baits.

"Thanks," I said. "I'll be sure to take the DNR officer fishing with me...and a grandkid or two!"

A defense attorney appeared in court one very busy morning wearing a beautiful, expensive new suit. Other attorneys ragged on him, each trying to guess the suit's label. The consensus was "Pierre Cardin." The attorney tried to ignore their jabs and went in the hall with the prosecutor to work out a reduction in charges against his client.

When he appeared before me later in the day, I took a look at the many serious charges that had been dropped against his client as a result of the hall wrangling.

"Wow!" I observed. "The guessing is over. Your suit was made by Houdini!"

[Aside from Karen: the following is John's last keynote speech at the annual Peace Officers Memorial Day commemoration, Flint Memorial Park, May 15ᵗʰ, 2014]

Good morning—years ago, as a young judge, I remember standing here in a drizzling rain—a cold gray day—listening to Judge Gerald Snodgrass make his final appearance at this event. It was Judge Snodgrass, along with John Nickola, Ed Smith, Bud Schaaf and others, who started this tradition of honoring fallen officers…a tradition that has now spread throughout the state of Michigan, and the country.

And while Judge Snodgrass was speaking, it flashed through my mind that someday—someday, God willing, I would be standing here making MY final official appearance. Well, folks, the days since then have sometimes been long, but the years have been fleeting. And that someday has come.

So, in light of that, I would just quickly share a personal note to the officers and families here today. I want to thank you. It has been an honor and privilege to serve you for more than twenty years…to call you friends. As the years have passed, I've grown to have even more appreciation for you and your families…to share in your daily anxieties as our own son steps out every night as an officer into the streets of a troubled, crime-ridden city while his family prays for his safety.

So, once again, we are here to honor our fallen officers—our heroes. But we are also here to honor their families and the living officers who sacrifice every day to make their communities safe. We do this because in today's world we have a rediscovery of courage as a virtue—and the most courageous people give of themselves, even in the face of danger—police officers, firefighters, soldiers. We ask them to defend us against criminals, terrorists, thugs, and natural disasters.

And when the dreadful possibility of death turns into reality, the fallen officers deserve our sincere homage to the sacrifice they have made. When an officer dies in the line of duty, he has given him or herself for the way of life that you and I take for granted: the safe streets, our safe homes, our knowledge that help is close at hand in an emergency.

But for all our gratitude for these sacrifices, there are others who suffer sacrifice too: the little boys and girls who will never get to play catch or fish with dad or mom. There will always be a missing aunt or uncle or grandparent at the family table. Someone's applause will be missing at dance recitals, and someone's embrace will be missing at that special occasion.

The surviving spouse must face the stark realities of raising the kids, maybe going back to work, paying the bills in a difficult economy, and dealing with the grief and anger. This is when these wonderful people dig way down to find their own courage…the courage to wake up each day and tackle their responsibilities with dignity.

And despite everything, the badge carries on. It wears a different face, a different name, but the danger is always the same. That officer places his or her life on the line, while we peacefully carry on with our own lives. They place their lives on the line every time they open that car door; every time they are called to make a run; every time they give chase: a radar gun is not a crystal ball. We are here to honor those living heroes who respond to the call of an often dangerous, demanding, gut-wrenching job… and they respond because they know the rewards of keeping our communities safe.

They are also, just like us, moms, dads and grandparents.

They do all of the things we like to do. But, contrary to most of us, they miss holidays, school events, recitals, baseball games, and often a lot of sleep! And on top of everything else, their job is to provide positive role models—through schools, churches, coaching, mentoring—anyway they can make a difference in the lives of young men and women before trouble begins.

Every year, after this ceremony, I walk away—carrying a coffee cup—tents are coming down—and I trudge through the spring grass toward my car. The bagpipes are done blowing—the color guard is gone, and the sound of silence takes over for another year.

The fallen heroes go back to their resting place—and the living heroes, both officers and family survivors, head back to the business of living. It is with Amazing Grace that the Brotherhood carries on. They carry on today, for in tomorrow lies our hope for a safe community for our children. The men and women behind the badge give us that hope.

The men and women that we remember today, honored us with their lives. It is with humility and reverence that we pay honor to their memories.

We thank God for those who choose to be police officers. They deserve a fair chance. They deserve to live—and so they do live—in our thoughts—in our fondest and cherished memories—and in our fervent prayers for a safer and kinder world. The fallen officers' noble sacrifice of their yesterdays gives us the promise for that better tomorrow that is the vision of every caring citizen.

It's been a great run. But the time is now: time for me to ease on down the road. Thanks for allowing me to be part of the Brotherhood. I wear it as a badge of honor.

You've probably noticed, my reader friend, there's a little sadness in all of these funny stories. As I get older, I can see clearly that it applies to life in general, and none of us escapes that fact (not even Houdini!).

As I approach retirement, I'm reminded of a friend of ours who, for many years, was a kindergarten building principal in our community.

She announced her retirement to an assembly of teachers and a couple hundred perplexed small children who were not really sure what Mrs. Hynes was talking about. After the assembly, as she was walking back to her office, a little boy tugged on her hand: "Mrs. Hynes," he said as he glanced up at her. "Are you going away *forever?*"

"Oh no, Billy," she smiled down at him. "I'll come back and visit once in a while."

"Ohhhh," Billy said with five-year-old wisdom that knows a little too much of life: "Rehab, huh?"

So…off I go to Rehab with all the other retirees, and hope that I learn something useful so I can keep contributing to the lives of others, as God gives me opportunity….